Stories i.

Our Heritage of Evidence

"What mean ye by these stones?
...These stones shall be for a memorial
unto the children..."
Joshua 4: 6-7

Tim Schmig

1

Stories in Stones
© Tim Schmig 2020

This book started from notes and memories of trips I conducted for various groups. In the process of production I reference other sources to supplement the content.

Most photographs are mine unless otherwise attributed.

Layout and formatting advice by Melissa Barker

Cover design by Mark Chartier

Copyright © 2017 Tim Schmig
2nd Printing April 2020
3rd Printing October 2020

ISBN: 978-154-874-3321
ISBN—781548-743321

Cover Photo: Tim Schmig
Back Cover photo: Jacob Elwart

"Nullius in verba"

Motto of the Royal Society
"Take nobody's word for it."
(See for yourself)

What others have said about Tim's tours:

"Great! Love Tim's stories and remembrances. Can't wait for his book to come out."

"Tim is an amazing tour guide and knows his stuff! You can tell that he has done research for all of the places we've seen!"

"Wonderful, godly man. Very informative. Tim is very intelligent and knowledgeable. What a guy!! God bless you!!"

"Very sensitive to group and environment. So knowledgeable. I would recommend others to take any educational trip. I will look at history with a better mind set. Loved this tour."

"Passionate for our country and even more so for our Lord."

"Very knowledgeable and accommodating. A good story teller who can wear his humility on his sleeve."

"Extremely interesting--able to make the slow commutes very interesting and informative."

"Tim is very knowledgeable and funny. Made the trip great."

"Tim is very knowledgeable about the places we visited. He also takes us to places that are off the beaten path, but relevant to our heritage of our Founding Fathers. Excellent."

"Excellent! He needs to write his own books so we know we are getting the true story."

"Second time having Tim for a tour guide. Second to none, in my opinion."

"Top notch. Beautifully done. A wealth of knowledge, stories. Emphasis on Christ throughout. Directed us with an understanding of particular needs. Led with grace."

"Tim is knowledgeable about what we were learning and he explained our history from the spiritual aspect with it. He did an excellent job. He also showed Christian character and that added to my experience of this trip."

"Tim is very knowledgeable about the Christian perspective of history. It was great to have him as a guide!"

"Easy-going, informative, understandable. Liked the view of America and our history from a Christian perspective."

"I love Tim as a tour guide. Thank you for making history come alive! Excellent."

"Thank you for all the behind the scenes information. I never learned that in history class."

"Very focused and often reminded us of purpose of this Christian heritage theme wherever we went."

"He was awesome!!! Can't say enough and I would definitely do one of his tours again."

"Tim is a great guide. Patient with folks of all ages and able to make the tour touch the lives of all who participate. He is flexible and knows a good balance to teach and allow folks to discover for themselves. Great trip!"

"For the past eight years, I have had the extraordinary opportunity of observing and listening to Dr. Tim Schmig guide my sixth grade class on a three-day tour of our nation's capital and George Washington's Mt. Vernon home.

My students eagerly count down the days to the start of the trip and return excited with the knowledge they have gained about the Bible's influence in their country's history and the life stories of many famous Americans during our tour.

Our school parents typically plan years in advance to join their children on the Washington DC tour so they don't miss the opportunity to hear Dr. Schmig's rich historical and biblical narrative. Through this book you will benefit from the author's expertise and passion to tell the story of the great influence the Bible has had on our country's foundation and leaders."

Karen Black

Bethany Christian School, Troy, MI

"I have always thoroughly enjoyed and benefited personally from Tim's breadth and depth of knowledge regarding the founding of our nation. His tireless work to understand the meaning of the American founding has led to his ability to passionately and effectively communicate these ideas and beliefs. His *Stories in Stones* are enduring reminders of the shared heritage that our national monuments are intended to convey. Enjoy his presentation of these stories as - in the spirit of Lincoln's words - the 'mystic cords of memory swell within you … touched by the better angels of our nature.' "

Jamison Coppola AACS Legislative Director Washington, D.C.

"We've travelled to Washington D.C. twice with Tim Schmig and we were thrilled to see our nation's heritage with Scripture carved into stone in the granite monuments of our Capitol."

Randy Melchert Jr.

VCY Radio Milwaukee, Wisconsin

"Our Connecticut church family took a motor-coach trip to Washington, DC for a "Stories In Stones Tour" conducted by tour-guide extraordinaire, Tim Schmig. Our seventy-one passengers (ranging from all ages), were thoroughly entertained, educated, and most of all, inspired, as to our Nation's Christian heritage, as we visited the White House, the Jefferson and Lincoln memorials, along with Arlington National Cemetery and Mount Vernon. Tim shared golden nuggets of our Nation's history that, sadly, has been virtually expunged by the average, politically correct, government employed, park ranger/ historian. "If the foundations be destroyed, what..." Tim Schmig's love for his Lord and country makes him a highly capable American Christian historian of the first degree."

Pastor Marty Shott

Harvest Baptist Church New Hartford, CT

"I have known Tim Schmig for many years and have had the pleasure of visiting many historical locations with him. We have gone to Washington D.C., New York City, Philadelphia, Baltimore, Gettysburg, and Valley Forge, as well as several other sites. On every trip, his historical and biblical knowledge has made history come alive, and helped me to see the hand of God in the founding and keeping of our great nation. I believe you will find that same kind of historically accurate and exciting information in his writing as well."

Pastor Brett Sharp

Freedom Baptist Church, Glenolden, PA

"*Stories in Stones* is a must-see presentation for every believer who cherishes the godly heritage we enjoy here in America. Dr. Schmig provides his audience with a wide variety of information demonstrating Christianity's impact upon the birth of our nation. He accomplishes this task by citing passages from our country's founding documents, quoting our founding fathers, and capturing visual evidence of the many Biblical references in locations throughout Washington, DC. In doing so, he silences the objections of the anti-God and anti-Bible crowd who shamelessly promote their secular agenda in their relentless effort to re-write our history. One would be hard pressed to find a better summary of why America is such a God blessed land."

Dr. Gene Krachenfels, Pastor,

Temple Baptist Church, Sarasota, FL

"George Washington's famous farewell address declared that "religion and morality are indispensable supports" to the political prosperity and the overall happiness of the American people. After almost two and a half centuries, our first president's words have proved to be almost prophetic. Our nation's unfolding history has consistently demonstrated that faith in God has indeed been an essential pillar keeping our nation safe and strong. Both those who made American history and those who recorded it have recognized the gracious working of God. For the current generation, understanding the place of religion in our nation's past remains a vital element in encouraging both godliness and liberty for the present and the future.

Tim Schmig hosted a tour of the nation's capital for two dozen members of the church I pastor. He skillfully pointed out testimonies of faith engraved in government buildings and monuments. From well known sites such as the

Supreme Court building and the Lincoln and Jefferson Memorials to little-known plaques and statues, we were shown countless monuments that recorded not only human history but also divine providence and praise to God. The tour not only enhanced our knowledge of American history, it profoundly encouraged our faith as Christians.

Whether in the role of tour guide, lecturer, educator, or author, Tim Schmig's presentation of Stories in Stones is an invaluable resource to preserve and promote American heritage and faith in God. His work strengthens those 'indispensable supports' on which our country rests."

Dr. David Oliver, Pastor

Ashley Baptist Church, Belding, MI

"I had the privilege of accompanying Tim Schmig on a tour of Washington D.C. My eyes were opened as never before to our great Christian heritage in the founding of our country. Everywhere we visited, I was amazed as Tim brought my attention to the many statues and monuments inscribed with Biblical values and the Word of God. His skill in sharing key historical facts to accompany these sites gave insight that could never have been gained on a casual visit. Tim's knowledge of events and people from our history proved to be a deeply moving experience and drove me to worship the Lord in appreciation for His goodness in the founding of our great country."

Pastor Dan White
Fellowship Baptist Church, Clarklake, MI

Stories in Stones

Tour Guide and Photographs

Dr. Tim Schmig

BA, MM, D.Litt

ACKNOWLEDGMENTS

I would like to thank the Congressmen and Congressional staffers who were patient with my requests for tours, sometimes after hours, to secure photographs of some of these treasures.

Additionally, I would like to thank those who left us these National Treasures because in our secular progressive society the history of monuments, manuscripts, men, and moments of our heritage is slowly being rewritten and forgotten. These photos need no explanation. They speak for themselves. However, at times I would like to add my own observations.

"Books will speak plain when counsellors Blanch."
Francis Bacon *Of Studies*

Special acknowledgement to dear friends who helped to bring this edition to print.

Phil Larsen, a friend and counsellor and someone I am eternally grateful for. Thank you for your observations and gentle suggestions.

Randy Melchert, my tour guide companion and prime mover to get me to put our Washington, D.C. tour guide information into print.

Melissa Barker, for offering advice with a jeweler's eye to detail.

Josh Blankenbaker, one of my main proof readers. You are always an encouragement.

Dr. Tim Schmig is the Executive Director of the Michigan Association of Christian Schools. He is blessed to be able to lead Christian Heritage tours of Washington, D.C. and other historic US Cities. All rights reserved. No part of this publication may be reproduced or transmitted in any form or by any means (you know what I mean) without written permission from Tim. This book is assembled from multiple sources over many years. During that time, websites have shutdown or have been moved and the ability to cite some of the information is lost beyond retrieval.

Indebtedness is extended to anyone who can find source or publication for any work used here and it will be corrected as we go forward with future printings. Contact me at timschmig@gmail.com

"You should write a book."

With that simple suggestion a seed thought was planted. I had thought of writing a book before, but really, about what? I thought if I ever did, I would want it to contribute to the dialogue of our Christian heritage and to be a help to others. For years I have been giving a presentation called *Stories in Stones* a simple power point tour of Washington, D.C. showing some of the highlights of the Bible verses in the monuments and other evidence pointing to a clear Judeo-Christian foundation in America.

My first trip to Washington, D.C. was in August of 1977 when we moved my future mother-in-law there to be Senator Hubert Humphrey's secretary. After getting her settled in her new town house, she took us to work with her to see the Senate Office building. She contacted a friend of hers who worked for Vice President Mondale and got us into the White House. Seeing the Oval Office and touring some of the Executive Mansion was an amazing experience. You might think the story of telling the story of our monuments would have begun there. For me, it didn't click until we were given a one day pass on the double-decker tour buses. You could hop on and hop off at any stop the whole day. Each bus had a guide that would comment on the tour and the sites around us. When we were headed to the Lincoln Memorial one guide commented on the reflecting pool and how he was told it came about. He said to the effect, that in the 1920s Washington, D.C. was a hot, humid town that was very uncomfortable to try to live in during the summers. So in a stroke, nothing short of genius, they thought if they could put a body of water in the middle of a public square it would act as some sort of air conditioner. As we sat on that bus in the hot sticky August afternoon the guide went on to ask, "How's that working out for ya?"

Since that day I have taken scores of trips to Washington, D.C. for my legislative time with both National Write Your Congressman and Michigan Association of Christian Schools. Usually on my legislative trips I will schedule one extra day to take the tours to see what they say because once in a while, I'm asked to guide a Christian School or church group. Truthfully, I have never heard another guide tell the reflecting pool story, sometimes they make it up as they go along. In putting this book together, I have researched everything so as to not be too guilty of embellishing. After all, we are here to tell a story.

So it is with this book. Every year, over 19 million people visit Washington, D.C. to go to the monuments and see the sites. Of those 19 million very few ever go to their politician's office. I think that is because the monuments are unchanging and rarely disappoint us as their story is graven in stone and besides, they are not running for re-election.

My desire to tell the story of the monuments began on a legislative trip to Washington, D.C. and I was thinking about what I had been told about the founding of our country. The Founders were not in any sense religious men, they were atheists, they did not believe in God. If they weren't atheists then surely they were agnostics, they did not know if you could know the truth. Finally, if they were neither of these, surely, they were Deists, God Created the world, but after that he had no personal contact with his creation. Atheists, Agnostics, and Deists? As I walked around the Nation's Capitol, I would see Bible verses on the monuments, statues of Moses, Daniel and the icon for the Ten Commandments and it dawned on me that the monuments were telling a different story than the commentators. This is the story of the monuments, the moments, the men and women, and the manuscripts of our heritage. This is our *Stories in Stones*.

Dedication

Stories in Stones is dedicated to my loving wife, Sue, who has been with me every step of the way. She has suffered my setbacks and celebrated our successes at every turn. Looking back over these years, she is always forbearing and has been an encouragement when I need it most. The wonderful thing about growing old together is the shared memories. She knows that I am susceptible to a good story and that I have a tendency to travel in familiar spaces. I don't like change, even though it is inevitable, and often times in more ways than one, I live in the past. "Guilty as charged, your Honor."

Because of my romantic inclinations, I have a tendency to be more familiar with what happened from 1760 to 1945 than with our current culture. Sue sees all of this and loves me anyway. Without her, I have no idea where I would have ended up in life. She is everything to me, because everything I am, and everything I hope to be, I owe to the Lord and that wonderful summer when I met her.

My Sue, one of the greatest gifts the Lord ever gave me was your friendship. Thank you for everything. I can say that the smartest thing I ever did was to marry you.

Stories In Stones

A Tour Guide's observations
 of Washington, D.C.
with an emphasis on our
Heritage of Evidence.

Washington, D.C.	Temperature Range	Rainy Days
March	35°- 56°	7
April	44°-67°	8
May	54°-76°	9
June	63°-85°	8
July	68°-89°	8
August	66°-87°	7
September	59°-81°	7
October	46°-69°	6
November	37°-59°	6

Packing Tips

Don't over pack, travel light and layer your clothing. I suggest that you have comfortable shoes as you will do quite a bit of walking and it is never a good idea to get a new pair of shoes for your time in Washington, D.C. On any give day it could rain so have a light rain jacket with you. Drink plenty of water and carry a water bottle with you. Always have a hat or head covering as you will be outside a lot. Carry a backpack with a few snacks or energy bars and fruit and nuts.

Bring your camera and take lots of pictures. You are making memories that will last a lifetime. Enjoy your time in our Nation's Capitol.

Did you know?

The purpose of this book is two-fold: to tell some of the stories found in our national monuments and to assist your tour of Washington, D.C.

Throughout this tour guide book you will find pages that look like this with a photo frame. These pages may have things for you to notice at the site or some other trivia for you as you tour Washington, D.C.

I trust that they will add to your enjoyment and anticipation of your visit and contribute to the memories you make while you are in our Nation's Capital.

Site: Arlington National Cemetery
Metro Stop: Arlington National Cemetery on the Blue Line

Our Heritage, as represented in our monuments is so powerful that when Ronald Reagan gave his first Inaugural Address in January of 1981, he concluded his remarks with these memorable words:

"On the eve of our struggle for independence a man who might have been one of the greatest among the Founding Fathers, Dr. Joseph Warren, President of the Massachusetts Congress, said to his fellow Americans, Our country is in danger, but not to be despaired of.... On you depend the fortunes of America. You are to decide the important questions upon which rests the happiness and the liberty of millions yet unborn. Act worthy of yourselves.

I am told that tens of thousands of prayer meetings are being held on this day, and for that I am deeply grateful. We are a nation under God, and I believe God intended for us to be free. It would be fitting and good, I think, if on each Inauguration Day in future years it should be declared a day of prayer.

This is the first time in history that this ceremony has been held, as you have been told, on this West Front of the Capitol. Standing here, one faces a magnificent vista, opening up on this city's special beauty and history. At the end of this open mall are those shrines to the giants on whose shoulders we stand.

Directly in front of me, the monument to a monumental man: George Washington, Father of our country. A man of humility who came to greatness reluctantly. He led America out of revolutionary victory into infant nationhood. Off to one side, the stately memorial to Thomas Jefferson. The Declaration of Independence flames with his eloquence.

And then beyond the Reflecting Pool the dignified columns of the Lincoln Memorial. Whoever would understand in his heart the meaning of America will find it in the life of Abraham Lincoln.

Beyond those monuments to heroism is the Potomac River, and on the far shore the sloping hills of Arlington National Cemetery with its row upon row of simple white markers bearing crosses or Stars of David. They add up to only a tiny fraction of the price that has been paid for our freedom.

Each one of those markers is a monument to the kinds of hero I spoke of earlier. Their lives ended in places called Belleau Wood, The Argonne, Omaha Beach, Salerno and halfway around the world on Guadalcanal, Tarawa, Pork Chop Hill, the Chosin Reservoir, and in a hundred rice paddies and jungles of a place called Vietnam.

Under one such marker lies a young man-- Martin Treptow--who left his job in a small town barber shop in 1917 to go to France with the famed Rainbow Division. There, on the western front, he was killed trying to carry a message between battalions under heavy artillery fire.
We are told that on his body was found a diary. On the flyleaf under the heading, My Pledge, he had written these words: America must win this war. Therefore, I will work, I will save, I will

sacrifice, I will endure, I will fight cheerfully and do my utmost, as if the issue of the whole struggle depended on me alone.

The crisis we are facing today does not require of us the kind of sacrifice that Martin Treptow and so many thousands of others were called upon to make. It does require, however, our best effort, and our willingness to believe in ourselves and to believe in our capacity to perform great deeds; to believe that together, with God's help, we can and will resolve the problems which now confront us. And, after all, why shouldn't we believe that? We are Americans. God bless you, and thank you." (1)

Whenever I take a tour group to Washington DC, Arlington National Cemetery is always on the list of required stops. Being here puts the trip in perspective. Here are buried 428,000+ soldiers, sailors, marines and airmen, men and women who wore the uniform and some giving the last full measure of devotion to insure the freedoms we enjoy.

For me it is just the visual of every direction where you look you see simple white markers over the graves of Fathers, Sons, Husbands, and Daughters, some of whom gave their tomorrows for our todays.

As you leave the visitor's center and head uphill on the road that will take you to either John F. Kennedy's grave or The Tomb of the Soldier Known to God, you will see this sign: *Welcome to Arlington National Cemetery our nation's most Sacred Shrine. At the bottom it reads, Please remember these are hallowed grounds.* Sacred Shrine, Hallowed Grounds, these are words you rarely hear from government officials.

British Prime Minister William Gladestone observed "Show me the method and manner a nation cares for its dead and I will measure with mathematical exactness their tender mercies and devotion to high ideals."

The concept of military cemeteries dates back to the times of the Greeks and Romans where they would bury their military dead outside of the city walls in formation as silent testimony to these men still guarding family and fortunes.

They would also bring back the remains of one fallen soldier unable to be identified and those remains would be interned with special ceremony.

General Patton is remarked to have said, "It is foolish and wrong to mourn the men who died, rather we should thank God that such men lived." Arlington National Cemetery is a place of dignity and respect.

Let me point out just a few of the things you will see as you make your way up to the Tomb of the Soldier Known to God. Just as you pass Weeks Road, stop by the knoll of headstones and look for Mike Mansfield. Mike was born in 1903 and when he was 14 years old he enlisted in the US Navy serving aboard the *USS Minneapolis* until it was discovered he was only 15 years old. Later he enlisted in the US Army and after 2 years he enlisted in the US Marine Corps.

His family moved to Montana where he worked in a men's clothing store. In 1942 he ran for the lone congressional seat from Montana and won, serving as their Congressman from 1943-1955. In 1954 he ran for the open Senate seat and won, serving as US Senator from 1955 to 1977. During his time in office, the Democrats were in control and he served as Senate majority leader. He was the longest serving Senate majority leader in the history of the United States. After he left the Senate, he was appointed our Ambassador to Japan, becoming the longest serving Ambassador to Japan in U.S history. He completed his public service to our country by being awarded the Medal of Freedom, the highest honor a U.S citizen can get from our country. With all of the accomplishments, notice the one thing he wanted to be remembered for: Private USMC.

Take the road to the left and you will head toward the changing of the guard. Just before you get to the walkway to the Tomb, look for a headstone that says Andersen. Do you see the Bible verse on it?

Turn up the walkway and start looking for a large brown headstone that says **Louis** on it. This is the marker for Joe Louis, the great boxer known as the Brown Bomber. He famously boxed Max Schmelling of Adolf Hitler's Germany.

When World War II broke out Joe Louis desired to serve his country, but being a national treasure, the best way he could serve was as a fundraiser for war bonds. There is a famous recruiting poster that would have appeared in recruiting centers, post offices and college classrooms that shows Joe Louis in his military uniform, rifle with fixed bayonet in the charge position and the caption under it reads: Private Joe Louis says... "We're going to do our part ...and we'll win because we're on God's side."

Make your way up the walkway and turn left toward the tomb. With reverence watch the dignified Honor Guard perform their solemn duty to stand guard over our honored dead. Twenty-one steps. Precisely timed. Thorough inspection of every new guard and total respect and devotion to detail. For the major wars, World Wars I and II and Korea, any mother whose son didn't return could comfort herself in the thought that maybe it is my son who is honored and guarded in the Tomb at Arlington.

What to look for: At the Tomb of the Soldier Known to God, watch the solemn ceremony of the changing of the Guard in all of the careful detail that a nation can bestow upon its fallen soldiers. This is an awe-inspiring visual of the tender mercies of a grateful nation. As you look at the Tomb notice this inscription

'Here Rests in Honored Glory an American Soldier Known but to God.' This is not just a sentimental admission of government trying to find the right words to say that would be appropriate for the occasion, but rather a public declaration that Christendom claims The One True God who knows the humanly unknowable.

Here Rests
in Honored Glory
an American Soldier
Known but to God

That is the God we serve. This site serves as hope for any soldier that no matter what, they won't be forgotten. As we have become a more secular nation, drifting from our founding principles, we have adapted the idioms that seem to sound good, but are not exactly accurate. The Tomb of the Unknown Soldier. We call it that, but look at the inscription on the front of the tomb graven in marble. You see we as nation are saying we know that the true God knows the identity of the soldier in honored repose.

Proceed behind the amphitheater to the small sidewalk and notice the grave of Audie Murphy, the well-known soldier of World War II. Too small to initially enlist due to his 5'4" stature, as the war progressed on, some enlistment restrictions were loosened (by 1943 the army wasn't examining eyes as much as they were counting them) he was eventually allowed to enlist in the US Army. Through valor under enemy fire he distinguished himself as a soldier's soldier.

A lingering image for any Arlington National Cemetery visitor — more than caissons bearing the soon-to-be-interred or even the white-gloved honor guard at the Tomb of the Unknown Soldier — is the perfect symmetry of alabaster headstones endlessly arrayed. This is no accidental assembly of headstones, they are ordered and spaced with intent. The stone sentinels give up their dead only on close inspection to visitors who leave pathways to gingerly step close and read the black lettering etched into marble.

"Christopher David Horton, Spc. U.S. Army, Afghanistan, Oct. 1, 1984, Sept. 9, 2011, Bronze Star, Purple Heart, Valiant Warrior, Fearless Sniper" are words on one of more than 900 graves from the Iraq and Afghanistan wars in the cemetery's Section 60.

For the dead — like Horton, killed in a hail of enemy AK-47 fire — the words are a spare summary of sacrifice; what Abraham Lincoln called "the last full measure of devotion."(2)

More than 428,000+ men and women are buried here. The epitaphs are reminders that ever since Union Army Pvt. William Henry Christman became the first to be buried here on May 13, 1864 — this place has always been less about grandeur, stone and protocol than about people.

Navy Secretary Ray Mabus touched on this theme before a congregation at an Arlington burial service for two sailors killed in war: "We are joined as

Lincoln again reminded us by 'the mystic chords of memory, stretching from every battlefield, and every patriot grave, to every living heart and hearthstone.'"

The Sailors' remains were recovered years earlier from the sunken wreckage of the USS Monitor, famed for battling a Confederate ironclad to a draw in 1862. As the Civil War dead were carried to their Arlington graves, hundreds gathered. Scattered throughout were sailors of today in dress uniforms eager to link with this moment, each crisply saluting from wherever they stood.

Arlington National Cemetery is about people. Every headstone represents a father, son, brother, husband, mother, daughter or sister. Each stone represents a life lived and in many instances lost too soon.

It was the bitterness of Quartermaster Gen. Montgomery Meigs that first led to the cemetery's creation. Angry that his former mentor, Robert E. Lee, had joined the rebellion and desperate for more space to bury the accumulating dead of the Civil War, Meigs recommended that the Lee estate overlooking Washington be turned into a graveyard. Burials had already begun by the time approval came through on June 15, 1864.

A century later, it was with a simple nod of her head that Jacqueline Kennedy acquiesced to the gravesite for her husband on the slope below the Lee Arlington House. She insisted that the assassinated president be laid to rest in a public, accessible place because "he belongs to the people." On March 3, 1963 President John F. Kennedy, accompanied by his wife and a journalist friend, Charles Bartlett, toured Arlington National Cemetery. Surveying the sweeping vista of Washington from Lee Mansion and environs, the president remarked,

"I could stay here forever." Eight months later, he would be buried near that same spot.

A half-century after President Kennedy's burial, it was the outpouring of grief by young widows, parents and battle buddies that led to the only consistent splash of color within 624 acres of cemetery — the balloons, childhood drawings, stuffed Easter bunnies and personal memorabilia left on the graves of Iraq and Afghanistan war dead.

The now-widely recognized Section 60 is a long stroll from popular tourist sites such as the Kennedy grave and the Tomb of the Unknown Soldier. Unlike the deceased retired military that make up most of the 27-30 burials that occur at Arlington each day, the dead of Section 60 were so young, that the grieving here is far more intense.

So it is a place where a grieving father may be seen laying prostrate on his son's grave or where a mother sits in a thunderous downpour unaware that her lawn chair is sinking into a softening earth. Those who mourn regularly have coalesced into a kind of club, but one that one mother conceded "nobody wants to be in." For visitors who stroll the walkways or ride the trolleys across the cemetery, there are more stories than a single trip can encompass.

Here are seven little-known facts about some of the people of Arlington National Cemetery:

- For decades, an area south of the cemetery was home to thousands of former slaves. They began filtering into the capital area shortly after Lincoln's Emancipation Proclamation, hundreds settling near Arlington House. Freedman's Village was born and thriving with a school, hospital and church until disbanded about 1900, the land eventually included in the cemetery. About 3,200 unmarked contraband graves remain.

- Among the more infrequent of headstones at Arlington are those with gold lettering against the white marble. There are 403. These signify that the buried service member received the highest valor award — a Medal of Honor. One of the more recent belongs to 19-year-old Army Spc. Ross McGinnis, who lowered himself onto a grenade thrown inside the Humvee he was riding in Iraq in 2006.

- When John F. Kennedy was assassinated, his younger brother, Robert, urged that the grave be adorned with a simple white cross. He was overruled by his brother's widow, Jackie. After Robert was assassinated five years later, he was laid to rest near his brother, the grave marked with a simple, white wooden cross.

- Among 16,000 Civil War dead buried at Arlington, including several hundred Confederate soldiers, is the son of cemetery founder Montgomery Meigs. Lt. John Rodgers Meigs died in a skirmish in October 1864. His father later had him re-interred at Arlington beneath a tomb depicting in statuary the lieutenant's death scene, his body laying in the mud amid trampling hoof-prints of Confederate horses.

- Amid the head-stone covered hills of Arlington is the grave of Gen. John "Black Jack" Pershing, who led U.S. forces in World War I. Nearby are two grandsons: John W. Pershing, an Army veteran who died 1998 and Richard W. Pershing, killed in Vietnam in 1968. Along the slopes of the hill are buried troops the elder Pershing commanded.

- Three of the seven service members depicted in the iconic Marine Corps Memorial, showing the flag raising on Iwo Jima, are buried at Arlington. Two, Ira Hayes and Rene Gagnon, survived the battle and lived to see the memorial built just outside the cemetery. The third, Michael Strank, was killed in combat six days after the famous AP photo that inspired the statue was taken.

- A very rare group at the cemetery are the 184 victims of the 9/11 attack on the Pentagon. They are represented as co-mingled, unidentified remains buried under a memorial. There are individual victim graves nearby. One person whose remains were never identified was a 3-year-old girl aboard American Airlines Flight 77 that struck the Pentagon. The site is in a distant southeast corner of the cemetery several hundred feet from the Pentagon. It is unique in Arlington to be buried so close to where death occurred, cemetery officials say.

On fame's eternal camping ground
Their silent tents are spread
And glory guards the solemn round
The bivouac of the dead

Mackinac Island Soldiers Cemetery

Did you know?

- An average of 25 burials are performed each day.
- There are about 8,500 trees at Arlington National Cemetery, in 300 different varieties.
- Two state champion trees reside in the cemetery, signifying that they are the largest trees of their species in Virginia.
- The first military burial occurred at Arlington National Cemetery in 1864, for Private William Christman.
- Those eligible to be buried at Arlington include active duty military and retired reservists, recipients of the military's highest honors, and former POWs.
- The Tomb of the Unknowns is guarded 24/7 by the best, most qualified members of the 3rd U.S. Infantry Regiment, also known as The Old Guard. Formed in 1784, The Old Guard is the oldest active-duty infantry unit in the Army.
- When you visit Arlington National Cemetery you may see coins atop the headstones. There is a significance to the coins. A penny means "I visited your gravesite. A nickel means I was in basic training with you. A dime means I served with you and a quarter means I was there when you lost your life.

Site: Women in Military Service for America Memorial
Metro Stop: Arlington National Cemetery on the Blue Line

The Women In Military Service For America Memorial (Women's Memorial) is the only major national memorial honoring all women who have defended America throughout history. We are proud to recognize their devoted patriotism and bravery as an integral part of our national heritage.

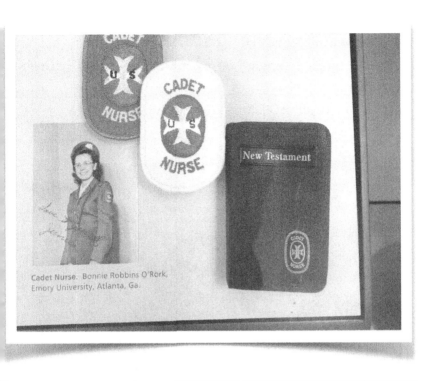

Cadet Nurse. Bonnie Robbins O'Rork, Emory University, Atlanta, Ga.

D.C Fun Fact: Washington, D.C was originally laid out as a 10 mile square. Mile markers were placed every mile and some of the markers are still standing in their original placement.

Northeast No. 2 Boundary Marker, along D.C./Maryland line, at 6980 Maple Street NW, Washington, D.C., with fence erected by the DAR.
(h/t) Jordana Coppola

Site: Marine Memorial

Metro Stops: Arlington on the Blue Line or Rosslyn on the Orange Line

What to look for: Six Boys And Twelve Hands

The Iwo Jima memorial is the largest bronze statue in the world and depicts one of the most famous photographs in history -- that of the six brave soldiers raising the American Flag at the top of Mount Suribachi on the island of Iwo Jima, Japan, during WW II.

Six boys raised the flag on February 23, 1945. The first guy putting the pole in the ground is Harlon Block.

Harlon was an all-state football player. He enlisted in the Marine Corps with all the senior members of his football team. They were off to play another type of game-a game called 'War.' But it didn't turn out to be a game. Harlon, at the age of 21, died with his intestines in his hands. I don't say that to gross you out, I say that because there are people who stand in front of this statue and talk about the glory of war. Most of the boys in Iwo Jima were 17, 18, and 19 years old - and it was so hard that the ones who did make it home never even would talk to their families about it.

You see this next guy? That's Rene Gagnon from New Hampshire. If you took Rene's helmet off at the moment this photo was taken and looked in the webbing of that helmet, you would find a photograph... a photograph of his girlfriend. Rene put that in there for protection because he was scared. He was 18 years old. It was just boys who won the battle of Iwo Jima. Boys. Not old men.

The next guy here, the third guy in this tableau, was Sergeant Mike Strank. Mike is my hero. He was the hero of all these guys. They called him the 'old man' because he was so old. He was already 24. When Mike would motivate his boys in training camp, he didn't say, 'Let's go kill some Japanese' or 'Let's die for our country.'

He knew he was talking to little boys. Instead he would say, 'You do what I say, and I'll get you home to your mothers.'

'The last guy on this side of the statue is Ira Hayes, a Pima Indian from Arizona. Ira Hayes was one of them who lived to walk off Iwo Jima. He went into the White House and President Truman told him, 'You're a hero.' He told reporters, 'How can I feel like a hero when 250 of my buddies hit the island with me and only 27 of us walked off alive?' Ira Hayes didn't see himself as a hero. Everyone thinks these guys are heroes, 'cause they are in a photo and on a monument'. Ira Hayes had images of horror in his mind and carried the pain home with him and eventually died dead drunk, face down, drowned in a very shallow puddle, at the age of 32.

The next guy, going around the statue, is Franklin Sousley from Hilltop, Kentucky. A fun-lovin' hillbilly boy, his best friend, told me, 'Yeah, you know, we took two cows up on the porch of the Hilltop General Store. Then we strung wire across the stairs so the cows couldn't get down. Then we fed them Epsom salts.' Yes, he was a fun-lovin' hillbilly boy. Franklin died on Iwo Jima at the age of 19. When the telegram came to tell his mother that he was dead, it went to the Hilltop General Store. A barefoot boy ran that telegram up to his mother's farm. The neighbors could hear her scream all night and into the morning. Those neighbors lived a quarter of a mile away.

The next guy is Harold Henry Schultz a United States Marine corporal who helped raise the second U.S. flag (a replacement flag) on top of Mount Suribachi on February 23, 1945, during the Battle of Iwo Jima in World War II. The Marine Corps announced on June 23, 2016, that Schultz is one of the flag-raisers in Joe Rosenthal's iconic photograph, Raising the Flag on Iwo Jima. The Marine Corps also stated after reviewing the identities of the six second-flag-raisers in the photograph that former Navy corpsman John Bradley who was thought to be in the photo since April 1945, was not. Schultz is the second flag-raiser in the photograph who was not originally identified as one. In 1947, after a Marine Corps investigation, it was determined that Corporal Harlon Block was in the photograph. The Marine Corps War Memorial in Arlington, Virginia, depicts the second flag-raising on Mount Suribachi by six Marines.

So that's the story about six nice young boys. Three died on Iwo Jima, and three came back as national heroes. Overall, 7,000 boys died on Iwo Jima in the worst battle in the history of the Marine Corps.

Suddenly, the monument wasn't just a big old piece of metal with a flag sticking out of the top. It came to life before our eyes with the heartfelt words of a son who did indeed have a father who was a hero. Maybe not a hero for the reasons most people would believe, but a hero nonetheless. (3)

We need to remember that God created this vast and glorious country for us to live in, freely, but also at great sacrifice. Let us never forget from the Revolutionary War to the current War on Terrorism and all the wars in-between that sacrifice was made for our freedom...please pray for our troops.

Take a moment to reflect and thank God for being alive and being free due to someone else's sacrifice. God Bless You and God Bless America.(2) Every day that we can wake up free, it's because of some brave men and women who wear the uniform were there to protect us.

Site: Supreme Court Building
Metro Stops: Union Station on the Red Line or Capitol South on the Blue/ Orange Line

This Magnificent study in architecture is the home of the highest court in the land. The Supreme Court has issued rulings that have dramatically affected American History. From the Dred Scott Case that many feel led to heightened tensions preceding the Civil War to *Roe v Wade* and the fallout socially and morally from that landmark case, The Court has been the center of much of the cultural controversy that we face today. The front of the Supreme Court Building is on the west side. Walk along the south side of the building between the Supreme Court and the Library of Congress on Capital Street NE until you come to the east side of the Supreme Court Building. Look up toward the apex of the pediment and you will see a Statue of Moses holding two tablets representing the Ten Commandments.

When you are in the Supreme Court Building you will see

two massive oak doors leading to the main chamber of the court room. Look closely at the doors and notice this panel in the door. I was giving a tour of Washington, D.C and was unable to stay with the group for the last day

and their tour of the Supreme Court. I asked the Pastor to ask the tour guide what this panel represented? That night he called me and said "You won't believe it, he said it represented the first 10 amendments to the Constitution." (Google "10 Commandments Icon" and see if he's right.)

In the main Chamber on the South wall is a frieze with Moses holding a tablet with commandments VI-X in Hebrew.

Every day they are in session, the Supreme Court's proceedings begin with *"Oyez! Oyez! Oyez!...* God save the United States and this honorable Court!"

Did you know?

- John Marshall is only one of two justices to appear on U.S. currency. Marshall was on the $500 bill, while Salmon P. Chase was on the $10,000 bill. Neither bill is in circulation today.

- Taft was the only former President to sit on the Court, but not the only presidential candidate. Taft died before the new Supreme Court building was opened and he is still the only president who later became a Justice. So unpleasant was his term as President of the United States that late in life he remarked "I don't ever recall being President."

- The Court really didn't have a fully functional home until 1935. The Court was in various locations before the Civil War, and it was housed in the Old Senate Chamber from 1861 to 1935. The chamber wasn't spacious; the Justices ate lunch in the robing room. Chief Justice William Howard Taft led the drive for a Supreme Court building in the 1920s.

- Eight future Supreme Court justices clerked at the Supreme Court: Byron R. White, William H. Rehnquist, John Paul Stevens, Stephen G. Breyer, John G. Roberts, Elena Kagan, Neil Gorsuch, and Brett Kavanaugh.

Site: The Capitol Building

Metro Stops: Union Station on the Red Line or Capitol South on the Blue/ Orange/ Silver Line

What to look for: The U.S. Capitol also bears public witness to the legacy of Biblically inspired faith that Americans have passed on from generation to generation. New England statesman and orator Daniel Webster was voted by the United States Senate in the 1980s as one of the five greatest senators ever to serve in that chamber. In

1851, when the new House and Senate wings of the Capitol were begun, Webster gave a speech that was deposited in the cornerstone. Its final words are these:

"If, therefore, it shall hereafter be the will of God that this structure should fall from the base, that its foundations be upturned, and this deposit brought to the eyes of men, be it then known, that on this day the Union of the United States of America stands firm, that their constitution still

exists unimpaired, and with all of its original usefulness and glory, growing every day stronger and stronger in the affection of the great body of the American people, and attracting more and more the admiration of the world. And all here assembled, whether belonging to public life or to private life, with hearts devotedly thankful to Almighty God for the preservation of the liberty and happiness of the country, unite in sincere and fervent prayers that this deposit, and the walls and arches, the domes and towers, the columns and the entablatures, now to be erected over it, may endure forever."

The Visitors Center

Our National Motto in a Congressman's office

In the Dirkson Senate office Building.

In God We trust as our National Motto

Did you Know?

• President Abraham Lincoln's Secretary of the Treasury Salmon Chase instructed James Pollock, Director of the Mint at Philadelphia, to prepare a motto, in a letter dated November 20, 1861:

Dear Sir: No nation can be strong except in the strength of God, or safe except in His defense. The trust of our people in God should be declared on our national coins. You will cause a device to be prepared without unnecessary delay with a motto expressing in the fewest and tersest words possible this national recognition.

• The motto disappeared from the five-cent coin in 1883, and did not reappear until production of the Jefferson nickel began in 1938.
• It also has appeared on all gold coins and silver dollar coins, half-dollar coins, and quarter-dollar coins struck since July 1, 1908.
• Since 1938, all United States coins bear the inscription.

Rostrum of the Speaker of House

This is where the President of the United States delivers his State of the Union address. Notice what you would see if our national media would widen the camera angle a little bit. Why do you think you have never seen this when the President is speaking? Could it be that it doesn't fit the narrative that we are a secular nation in no need of God?

Stained glass window in the Congressional Prayer Room. Depicting George Washington kneeling in prayer. Over his head "This Nation Under God" and the Bible verse "Preserve Me O God For in Thee Do I Put My Trust." Psalm 16:1

The open Bible in the Congressional Prayer Room.

The Rotunda Ceiling: Apotheosis of Washington.

The Rotunda, The Embarkment of the Pilgrims.

The group appears contemplative of what they are about to undertake as they pray for divine protection through their voyage; the words "God with us" are on the sail in the upper left corner. The figures at the center of the composition are William Brewster, holding the Bible; Governor Carver, kneeling with head bowed and hat in hand; and pastor John Robinson, with extended arms, looking Heavenward. Gathered around them are the men, women, and children emphasizing the importance of the family in the

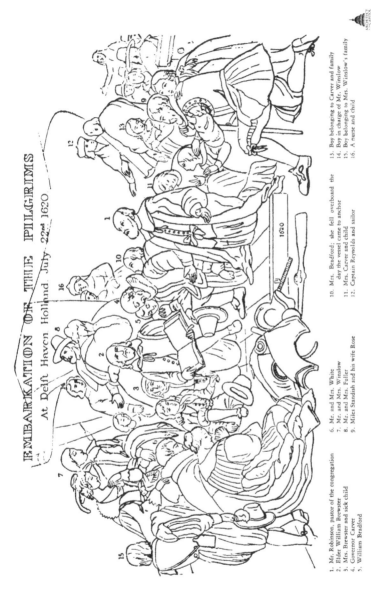

EMBARKATION OF THE PILGRIMS
At Delft Haven Holland July 22nd 1620

1. Mr. Robinson, pastor of the congregation
2. Elder William Brewster
3. Mrs. Brewster and sick child
4. Governor Carver
5. William Bradford
6. Mr. and Mrs. White
7. Mr. and Mrs. Winslow
8. Mr. and Mrs. Fuller
9. Miles Standish and his wife Rose
10. Mrs. Bradford; she fell overboard the day the vessel came to anchor
11. Mrs. Carver and child
12. Captain Reynolds and sailor
13. Boy belonging to Carver and family
14. Boy in charge of Mr. Winslow
15. Boy belonging to Mrs. Winslow's family
16. A nurse and child

69

lives of the Pilgrims. Some are dressed in traditional puritan attire while others wear more fanciful and bright garments. The armor, helmet, and musket in the foreground represent the tools that the Pilgrims will use for protection in the new and unfamiliar land. In the background on the left the rainbow represents the hope and promise of what lies ahead.

"God with us" on the sail over Mrs. Winslow.

The New Testament of our Lord and Saviour Jesus Christ (Photo turned 180° from painting)

Commenting on the contrast of stability and economic prosperity of North and South America, the President of Argentina said "South America was settled by the Spanish who went there in search of gold. North America was settled by the Pilgrims who went there in search of God." (4)

71

Next, look for the statue of Pastor Peter Muhlenberg who was authorized to raise and command as its colonel the 8th Virginia Regiment of the Continental Army. After George Washington personally asked him to accept this task, he agreed. However, his brother Fredrick Augustus Muhlenberg, who was also a minister, did not approve of him going into the army until the British burned down his own church in front of him. Then he joined the military himself. According to a biography written by his great nephew, on January 21, 1776 in the Lutheran church in Woodstock, Virginia, Reverend Muhlenberg took his sermon text from the third chapter of Ecclesiastes, which starts with *"To every thing there is a season..."*; after reading the eighth verse, *"a time of war, and a time of peace,"* he declared, "And this is the time of war," removing his clerical robe to reveal his Colonel's uniform.

Outside the church door the drums began to roll as men turned to kiss their wives and then walked down the aisle to enlist, and within half an hour, 162 men were enrolled. This statue depicts the moment he removed his ministerial robe underneath which he wore his uniform of the Virginia militia. He marched to the back of the church declaring to all, "if you do not choose to fight for your liberties, you will soon have no liberties to protect."

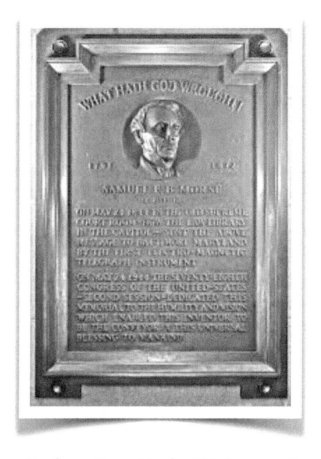

On the wall outside the Old Supreme Court Chamber is a bronze plaque honoring the inventor Samuel F. B. Morse. It commemorates the first long-distance telegraph message that he sent from the Capitol on May 24, 1844: "What Hath God Wrought." Morse had earlier demonstrated the telegraph by sending messages between the House and Senate Chambers, but it remained a question whether the device would work over any distance. Congress appropriated $30,000 to underwrite an experiment, and Morse strung wire along the Baltimore and Ohio railroad tracks from Washington to a station just outside of Baltimore. On May 24, 1844 a crowd gathered in the Supreme Court Chamber to watch Morse send the message —which a young woman had given him, sight unseen—and receive it back from Baltimore as confirmation. The words are a quote from the Bible: Numbers 23:23 *"Surely there is no enchantment against Jacob, neither is there any divination against Israel: according to this time it shall be said of Jacob and of Israel, What hath God wrought!"* The use of Morse's telegraphic invention grew rapidly and expanded not only across America but also the globe. Today we enjoy the modern technological blessings that sprang from what Christian inventor Samuel F. B. Morse had begun on May 24, 1844. (5)

Outside the Capitol on the west side is the Peace Monument. At the top of the Peace Monument, facing west, stand two classically robed female figures. Mercy holds her covered face against the shoulder of History and weeps in mourning for when history writes mercy is of no avail. History holds a stylus and a tablet that was inscribed, "They died that their country might live."

Below Mercy and History, another life-size classical female figure represents Victory, holding high a laurel wreath and carrying an oak branch, signifying strength.

Site: The Lincoln Memorial
Metro Stops: Foggy Bottom Georgetown on the
Orange line or Arlington on the Blue line, either
way, you have a walk to get there.

The life of Abraham Lincoln is going to get a little
more detail because of the significance of his
memorial and the importance of his life and
words to American History. Poet Robert Frost
said "Whoever would find in his heart the
meaning of America will find it in the life of
Abraham Lincoln." Carl Sandburg said Lincoln

was "the sad man musing on the role of Providence in the dust of events."

We are told that President Lincoln started his days by reading a few chapters from the Bible. He particularly liked the Psalms. "I find them best, I find something in them for every day of the year." After his assassination, as they were removing his affects from the executive mansion, when they picked up his Bible, it naturally fell open to Psalm 34. Knowing what you know about the Civil War and Abraham Lincoln's presidency, can you see why this Psalm might be of comfort and encouragement to him?

Psalm 34

I will bless the Lord at all times: his praise shall continually be in my mouth.

My soul shall make her boast in the Lord: the humble shall hear thereof, and be glad.

O magnify the Lord with me, and let us exalt his name together.

I sought the Lord, and he heard me, and delivered me from all my fears.

They looked unto him, and were lightened: and their faces were not ashamed.

This poor man cried, and the Lord heard him, and saved him out of all his troubles.

The angel of the Lord encampeth round about them that fear him, and delivereth them.

O taste and see that the Lord is good: blessed is the man that trusteth in him.

O fear the Lord, ye his saints: for there is no want to them that fear him.

The young lions do lack, and suffer hunger: but they that seek the Lord shall not want any good thing.

Come, ye children, hearken unto me: I will teach you the fear of the Lord.

What man is he that desireth life, and loveth many days, that he may see good?

Keep thy tongue from evil, and thy lips from speaking guile.

Depart from evil, and do good; seek peace, and pursue it.

The eyes of the Lord are upon the righteous, and his ears are open unto their cry.

The face of the Lord is against them that do evil, to cut off the remembrance of them from the earth.

The righteous cry, and the Lord heareth, and delivereth them out of all their troubles.

The Lord is nigh unto them that are of a broken heart; and saveth such as be of a contrite spirit.

Many are the afflictions of the righteous: but the Lord delivereth him out of them all.

He keepeth all his bones: not one of them is broken.

Evil shall slay the wicked: and they that hate the righteous shall be desolate.

The Lord redeemeth the soul of his servants: and none of them that trust in him shall be desolate.

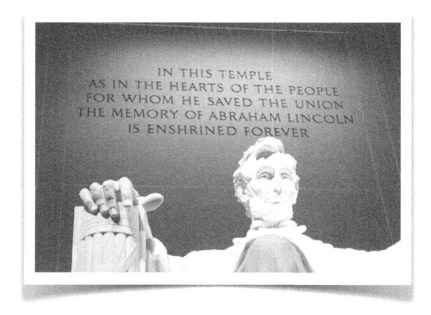

Lincoln is attributed with the first known use of "Michigander." In 1848, he used it derisively to describe former Michigan Territorial Governor Lewis Cass. Michiganian is the preferred term for those who know.

On February 11, 1861, newly elected President Abraham Lincoln delivered a Farewell

Speech to his home state in Springfield, Illinois, as he left for Washington, D.C.: "I now leave, not knowing when or whether ever I may return, with a task before me greater than that which rested upon Washington. Without the assistance of that Divine Being who ever attended him, I cannot succeed. With that assistance I cannot fail. Trusting in Him who can go with me, and remain with you, and be everywhere for good, let us confidently hope that all will yet be well.... "Unless the great God who assisted him shall be with me and aid me, I must fail: but if the same

omniscient mind and mighty arm that directed and protected him shall guide and support me, I shall not fail – I shall succeed. Let us all pray that the God of our fathers may not forsake us now. To him I commend you all. Permit me to ask that

with equal sincerity and faith you will invoke his wisdom and guidance for me."

Atop the steps of this memorial will offer you a great view of the Reflecting Pool and the Washington Monument. Inside this great memorial, note that over Abraham Lincoln's head they refer to this site as a Temple.

One notices that the statue of Lincoln can almost define his presidency in the manner of his body language. The left hand tight and the leg close to his body, the right hand open and the leg relaxed. As if the left side reflects the tension of the Civil War years and the right side, that brief moment of relief when the war ended.

On MAY 30, 1922, dedicating the Lincoln Memorial, Washington, D.C., President Warren G. Harding stated:

"In every moment of peril...there is the image of Lincoln to rivet our hopes and to renew our faith....He treasured the inheritance handed down by the founding fathers, the Ark of the Covenant wrought through their heroic sacrifices....Lincoln came almost as humbly as The Child of Bethlehem. His parents were unlettered, his home was devoid of every element of culture and refinement. He was no infant prodigy, no luxury facilitated or privilege hastened his development, but he had a God-given intellect, a love for work, a willingness to labor and a purpose to succeed."

Off to the side that is on Abraham Lincoln's right hand side you will see his Gettysburg Address. This short memorable speech mirrors the cadence of the King James Bible. Four score and seven years ago resonates like "Our Father which art in Heaven."

The brevity and poignancy makes this speech a classic for the ages. One writer wrote a book entitled the *Gospel at Gettysburg*. Lincoln says, 'the world will little note nor long remember what we say here.' There is historic irony right there. Famed orator of his day

Edward Everett spoke for two hours before Lincoln and next to nobody knows it or remembers one word he said. Almost every school child can recite the parts of Lincoln's Gettysburg Address.

Note that he says, 'This Nation Under God.' There is a concerted effort in some quarters of our land to have any such reference removed from the public square.

The Phrase 'Government of the people, by the people, for the people' could be a paraphrase of Wycliffe's preface to his Bible.

Lincoln's attitude toward the Scriptures can be summed up in this quote, "In regard for this great book I have this to say, it is the best gift God has given to man. All the good Saviour gave to the world was communicated through this book."

On Abraham Lincoln's left hand side you will see his Second Inaugural Address.

On March 4, 1865, Lincoln delivered his Second Inaugural Address considered by historians to be the most theological statement in American History. One writer said these are the words of "America's Theologian of Anguish." This masterpiece of speech is replete with scriptural reference allusions containing numerous acknowledgments of God and citations of Bible verses, including the declarations that "we here highly resolve that . . . this nation under God . . . shall not perish from the earth;" "The Almighty has His own purposes. 'Woe unto the world because of offenses; for it must needs be that offenses come, but woe to that man by whom the offense cometh' (Matthew 18:7);" "as was said three thousand years ago, so still it must be said 'the judgments of the Lord are true and righteous altogether' (Psalms 19:9);" "one day every valley shall be exalted and every hill and mountain shall be made low, the rough places will be made plain, and the crooked places will be made straight and the glory of the Lord shall be revealed and all flesh see it together."

This address, given just 45 days before his assassination, President Abraham Lincoln states: "Neither party expected for the war the magnitude or the duration which it has already attained…. Both read the same Bible and pray to the same God, and each invokes His aid against the other. It may seem strange that any men should dare ask a just God's assistance in wringing their bread from the sweat of other men's faces, but let us judge not, that we be not judged. The prayers of both could not be answered. That of neither has been answered fully. The Almighty has His own purposes… If we shall suppose that American slavery is one of those offenses which, in the providence of God…He now wills to remove, and that He gives to both North and South this terrible war as the woe due to those by whom the offense came…so still it must be said 'the judgments of the Lord are true and righteous altogether.'" Lincoln expressed that he believed the Civil War was part of God's wrath on the sin of slavery.

President Calvin Coolidge, on May 25, 1924, at the Confederate Memorial in Arlington National Cemetery, Virginia, stated:

"It was Lincoln who pointed out that both sides prayed to the same God. When that is the case, it is only a matter of time when each will seek a common end. We can now see clearly what that end is. It is the maintenance of our American ideals, beneath a common flag, under the blessings of Almighty God."

Did you Know?

Robert Taft Lincoln, son of President Lincoln, attended the dedication of the Lincoln Memorial in 1922.

In panel 1 of Lincoln's Second Inaugural Address, the mason was supposed to carve an "F" for the word Future and accidentally carved an "E." Even though they tried to cover the mistake, it is still visible.

Aren't you thankful that when we make a mistake it isn't carved in stone?

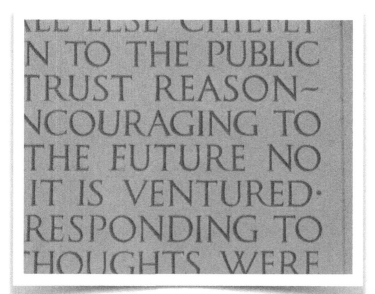

Fun Fact: If you have a five dollar bill and you walk about three fourths of the way down the reflecting pool towards the World War II memorial, you can capture a unique photograph.

Photo by Josh Frampton AACS

Did you know?

- There are 87 steps from the Reflecting Pool to Lincoln's statue in the monument. The number 87 represents 'four score and seven' as Abraham Lincoln spoke in his famous Gettysburg Address.
- The height of the Lincoln Memorial is 99 feet. The sculpture of the sitting Abraham Lincoln himself is 19 feet.
- The sculpture of Abraham Lincoln was designed by Daniel Chester French, who also designed Concord, Massachusetts' 'Minute Man' sculpture; and 'John Harvard' at Harvard University.
- At the time of Abraham Lincoln's death there were 36 states of the Union. This is the reason that there were 36 columns designed into the Lincoln Memorial.
- Abraham Lincoln's involvement in abolishing slavery led to the Lincoln Memorial becoming an important symbol for race relations. Martin Luther King gave his 'I Have a Dream' speech on the steps of the Lincoln Memorial on August 28th, 1963.
- The Lincoln Memorial is pictured on the back of the U.S. $5 bill and on one side of the U.S. penny.

Second Inaugural Address
by Abraham Lincoln

Fellow-Countrymen:

At this second appearing to take the oath of the Presidential office there is less occasion for an extended address than there was at the first. Then a statement somewhat in detail of a course to be pursued seemed fitting and proper. Now, at the expiration of four years, during which public declarations have been constantly called forth on every point and phase of the great contest which still absorbs the attention and engrosses the energies of the nation, little that is new could be presented. The progress of our arms, upon which all else chiefly depends, is as well known to the public as to myself, and it is, I trust, reasonably satisfactory and encouraging to all. With high hope for the future, no prediction in regard to it is ventured.

On the occasion corresponding to this four years ago all thoughts were anxiously directed to an impending civil war. All dreaded it, all sought to avert it. While the inaugural address was being delivered from this place, devoted altogether to *saving* the Union without war, insurgent agents were in the city seeking to *destroy* it without war—seeking to dissolve the Union and divide effects by negotiation. Both parties deprecated war, but one of them would *make* war rather than let the nation survive, and the other would *accept* war rather than let it perish, and the war came.

One-eighth of the whole population were colored slaves, not distributed generally over the Union, but localized in the southern part of it. These slaves constituted a peculiar and powerful interest. All knew that this interest was somehow the cause of the war. To strengthen, perpetuate, and extend this interest was the object for which the insurgents would rend the Union even by war, while the Government claimed no right to do more than to restrict the territorial enlargement of it. Neither party expected for the war the magnitude or the duration which it has already attained. Neither anticipated that the *cause* of the conflict might cease with or even before the conflict itself should cease. Each looked for an easier triumph, and a result less fundamental and astounding. Both read the same Bible and pray to the same God, and each invokes His aid against the other. It may seem strange that any men should dare to ask a just God's assistance in wringing their bread from the sweat of other men's faces, but let us judge not, that we be not judged. The prayers of both could not be answered. That of neither has been answered fully. The Almighty has His own purposes. "Woe unto the world because of offenses; for it must needs be that offenses come, but woe to that man by whom the offense cometh." If we shall suppose that American slavery is one of those offenses which, in the providence of God, must needs come, but which, having continued through His appointed time, He now wills to remove, and that He gives to both North and South this terrible war as the woe due to those by whom the offense came, shall we discern therein any departure from those divine attributes which the believers in a living God always ascribe to Him? Fondly do we hope, fervently do we pray, that this mighty scourge of war may speedily pass away. Yet, if God wills that it continue until all the wealth piled by the bondsman's two hundred and fifty years of unrequited toil shall be sunk, and until every drop of blood drawn with the lash shall be paid by another drawn with the sword, as was said three thousand years ago, so still it must be said "the judgments of the Lord are true and righteous altogether."

With malice toward none, with charity for all, with firmness in the right as God gives us to see the right, let us strive on to finish the work we are in, to bind up the nation's wounds, to care for him who shall have borne the battle and for his widow and his orphan, to do all which may achieve and cherish a just and lasting peace among ourselves and with all nations.

Abraham Lincoln

Site: New York Avenue Presbyterian Church

Metro Stops: McPherson Blue/ Orange or Silver or Metro Center Red Line

Located just two blocks from the White House, this is the church President and Mrs. Lincoln attended while they lived in Washington DC. The second pew on the right hand side is original from the days of the Civil War when the Lincoln's sat there for church services.

Above that pew on the balcony level you will see a stained glass window picturing the President in Church with his head bowed in prayer. This is an image the worshippers at church would have seen each week.

New York Avenue Presbyterian Church has played an important part in the history of Washington, D.C. Later the famed Chaplain, of the Senate Peter Marshall, would pastor this church.

Here is an excerpt from one of Peter Marshall's prayers that to me, is more timely and relevant today:

"The choice before us is plain: Christ or chaos, conviction or compromise, discipline or disintegration. I am rather tired of hearing about our rights and privileges as Americans. The time is come – it is now – when we ought to hear about the duties and responsibilities of our citizenship. America's future depends upon her accepting and demonstrating God's government."

At the laying of the cornerstone of the rebuilt New York Avenue Presbyterian Church, April 3, 1951, Rev. Peter Marshall's young son, Peter John Marshall, gave President Truman a New Testament, to which the President responded: "Well, thank you very much for this Testament. I appreciate very much having it. And all I can say to you is, I hope you will grow up to be as good a man as your father."

Did you know?

- Georgetown is the oldest part of the city, dating back to 1751 — 40 years before Washington, DC was founded.
- DC averages 39 inches of rainfall a year — more than Seattle!
- The Maine Avenue Fish Market has been operating nonstop since 1805, making it the oldest continuously functioning fish market in the country.
- William Smith, of South Carolina suggested the name of the new city at "the forks of the Potomac" be named Washingtonopolis.

Site: Thomas Jefferson Memorial
Metro Stops: Smithsonian on the Blue/Silver/ Orange Line or Arlington National Cemetery on the Blue Line

Composed of circular marble steps, a portico, a circular colonnade of Ionic order columns, and a shallow dome, the building is open to the elements. Architect John Russel Pope made references to the Roman Pantheon and Jefferson's own design for the Rotunda at the University of Virginia. It is situated in West Potomac Park, on the shore of the Tidal Basin of

the Potomac River. The Jefferson Memorial, and the White House located directly north, form one of the main anchor points in the area of the National Mall in D.C. The Washington Monument, just east of the axis on the National Mall, was intended to be located at the intersection of the White House and the site for the Jefferson Memorial to the south, but soft swampy ground which defied 19th century engineering required it be sited to the east.

The interior of the memorial has a 19-foot tall, 10,000 pound bronze statue of Jefferson by sculptor Rudulph Evans showing Jefferson looking out toward the White House, where he once lived. This statue was added four years after the dedication. Most prominent are the words which are inscribed in a frieze below the dome: "I have sworn upon the altar of God eternal hostility against every form of tyranny over the mind of man." This sentence is taken from a September 23, 1800, letter by Jefferson to Dr. Benjamin Rush wherein he defends the constitutional refusal to recognize a state religion. On the panel of the southwest interior wall are excerpts from the Declaration of Independence, written in 1776:

We hold these truths to be self-evident: that all men are created equal, that they are endowed by their Creator with certain inalienable rights, among these are life, liberty, and the pursuit of happiness, that to secure these rights governments are instituted among men. We...solemnly publish and declare, that these

WE HOLD THESE TRUTHS TO BE SELF-EVIDENT: THAT ALL MEN ARE CREATED EQUAL. THAT THEY ARE ENDOWED BY THEIR CREATOR WITH CERTAIN INALIENABLE RIGHTS. AMONG THESE ARE LIFE, LIBERTY AND THE PURSUIT OF HAPPINESS. THAT TO SECURE THESE RIGHTS GOVERNMENTS ARE INSTITUTED AMONG MEN. WE··· SOLEMNLY PUBLISH AND DECLARE, THAT THESE COLONIES ARE AND OF RIGHT OUGHT TO BE FREE AND INDEPENDENT STATES···AND FOR THE SUPPORT OF THIS DECLARATION, WITH A FIRM RELIANCE ON THE PROTECTION OF DIVINE PROVIDENCE, WE MUTUALLY PLEDGE OUR LIVES, OUR FORTUNES AND OUR SACRED HONOUR.

colonies are and of right ought to be free and independent states...And for the support of this declaration, with a firm reliance on the protection

ALMIGHTY GOD HATH CREATED THE MIND FREE. ALL ATTEMPTS TO INFLUENCE IT BY TEMPORAL PUNISHMENTS OR BURTHENS···ARE A DEPARTURE FROM THE PLAN OF THE HOLY AUTHOR OF OUR RELIGION···NO MAN SHALL BE COMPELLED TO FREQUENT OR SUPPORT ANY RELIGIOUS WORSHIP OR MINISTRY OR SHALL OTHERWISE SUFFER ON ACCOUNT OF HIS RELIGIOUS OPINIONS OR BELIEF, BUT ALL MEN SHALL BE FREE TO PROFESS AND BY ARGUMENT TO MAINTAIN, THEIR OPINIONS IN MATTERS OF RELIGION. I KNOW BUT ONE CODE OF MORALITY FOR MEN WHETHER ACTING SINGLY OR COLLECTIVELY.

of divine providence, we mutually pledge our lives, our fortunes, and our sacred honour.

Note that the inscription uses the word "inalienable," as in Jefferson's draft, rather than "unalienable," as in the published Declaration.

On the panel of the northwest interior wall is an excerpt from "A Bill for Establishing Religious Freedom, 1777." Except for the last sentence, the rest of the quote is taken from a letter of August 28, 1789, to James Madison:

"Almighty God hath created the mind free...All attempts to influence it by temporal punishments or burthens...are a departure from the plan of the Holy Author of our religion...No man shall be compelled to frequent or support any religious worship or ministry or shall otherwise suffer on account of his religious opinions or belief, but all men shall be free to profess and by argument to maintain, their opinions in matters of religion. I know but one code of morality for men whether acting singly or collectively."

The quotes from the panel of the northeast interior wall are from multiple sources. The first sentence, beginning "God who gave...," is from

"A Summary View of the Rights of British America." The second, third and fourth sentences

GOD WHO GAVE US LIFE GAVE US LIBERTY. CAN THE LIBERTIES OF A NATION BE SECURE WHEN WE HAVE REMOVED A CONVICTION THAT THESE LIBERTIES ARE THE GIFT OF GOD? INDEED I TREMBLE FOR MY COUNTRY WHEN I REFLECT THAT GOD IS JUST, THAT HIS JUSTICE CANNOT SLEEP FOR-EVER. COMMERCE BETWEEN MASTER AND SLAVE IS DESPOTISM. NOTHING IS MORE CERTAINLY WRITTEN IN THE BOOK OF FATE THAN THAT THESE PEOPLE ARE TO BE FREE. ESTABLISH THE LAW FOR EDUCATING THE COMMON PEOPLE. THIS IT IS THE BUSINESS OF THE STATE TO EFFECT AND ON A GENERAL PLAN.

are from Notes on the State of Virginia. The fifth sentence, beginning "Nothing is more…," is from Jefferson's autobiography. The sixth sentence, beginning "Establish the law…," is from an August 13, 1790, letter to George Wythe. The final sentence is from a letter of January 4, 1786, to George Washington:

"God who gave us life gave us liberty. Can the liberties of a nation be secure when we have removed a conviction that these liberties are the gift of God? Indeed I tremble for my country when I reflect that God is just, that his justice cannot sleep forever. Commerce between master and slave is despotism. Nothing is more certainly written in the book of fate than these people are to be free. Establish the law for educating the common people. This it is the business of the state to effect and on a general plan."

The two most stately monuments in all of Washington, D.C. are the Jefferson Memorial and the Lincoln Memorial. They capture the magnitude and grandeur of these men on the American landscape. Both are architectural testimonies of another era.

The most recent monuments have been monumental disappointments in their reach for political correctness- FDR in a wheelchair without his ubiquitous cigarette or the MLK memorial with its manufactured quotes that had to be redone because of public outcry.

Did you know?
Japan sent the Cherry Blossom trees to the U.S. to represent goodwill. In 1915, we reciprocated by sending flowering dogwood trees to Japan.

Please note the following letter from a pre-Presidential Abraham Lincoln on the importance of Thomas Jefferson.

Springfield, Ills, April 6, 1859
Messrs. Henry L. Pierce, & others.

All honor to Jefferson--to the man who, in the concrete pressure of a struggle for national independence by a single people, had the coolness, forecast, and capacity to introduce into a merely revolutionary document, an abstract truth, applicable to all men and all times, and so to embalm it there, that to-day, and in all coming days, it shall be a rebuke and a stumbling-block to the very harbingers of re-appearing tyranny and oppression.

Your obedient Servant
A. Lincoln--

Site: Washington Monument

Metro Stop: Smithsonian Blue/Orange/ Silver Line

What to look for: This is 555 feet tall and a monument to a monumental man. He is the Father of our Country. "First in War, First in Peace, First in the Hearts of his Countrymen." Though you can no longer take the elevator to the top and walk the steps down from the top of the Washington Monument, it is still an impressive visual monument. Descending the steps, one could notice messages engraved in the

stones including numerous Bible verses and religious acknowledgements carved on stones in the walls, including the phrases: "Holiness to the Lord" (Exodus 28:26; 30:30; Isaiah 23:18,

Zechariah 14:20),and "In God We Trust," One stone reads "May Heaven to this Union continue its beneficence." Along these walls you would read stones that said "Under the auspices of Heaven and the precepts of Washington, Kentucky will be the last to give up the Union" and "The Memory of the Just is Blessed" (Proverbs 10:7) and another that shows an open Bible with "Search the Scriptures." (John 5:39)

Atop the Monument in the aluminum pyramidion are inscribed the words "Laus Deo" Praise be to God. Every morning when the first rays of sunshine touch the monument they shine on the thought of praise be to God. In architecture, when the designer wants to make a statement of the future or looking ahead, he will put a statue or saying on the west side of a building. To place a symbol or saying on the east side is reflection on the past or what brought us to this point. In America we need to reflect on our history with praise be to God.

(Photos by Theodor Horydczak.)

Did you know?

- When the Washington Monument opened in 1884 it was the tallest structure in the world, until the Eiffel Tower in Paris took the title in 1889.

- No building in Washington D.C. is allowed to be taller than Washington Monument.

- The trowel that was used to lay the cornerstone of the Washington Monument in 1848 was the same trowel George Washington used to lay the cornerstone of the capitol in 1793.

- It took 30 years to build the Washington Monument. It was finished in 1884 but it didn't open until 1888. Construction had to be stopped during the Civil War.

- You see two different colors of stones in the Washington Monument because when the Civil War ended and construction began again, 20 years after it stopped, the quarry stone couldn't be matched like the stone they had before.

Site: Department of Agriculture Building
Metro Stop: Smithsonian Blue/Orange / Silver Lines

What to look for: On May 15, 1862, President Abraham Lincoln established the independent Department of Agriculture to be headed by a Commissioner without cabinet status. Lincoln called it the "people's department." On the front of this building you will see the verse "The laborer is worthy of his hire." I Timothy 5:18

Site: Old Post Office Pavilion and Clock Tower, Now Trump International Hotel
Metro Stop: Smithsonian Blue/Orange/ Silver Lines

The building is an example of Richardsonian Romanesque, part of the Romanesque Revival architecture of the nineteenth century United States. It is the third-tallest building in the national capital of Washington, D.C. Its 315-foot high Clock Tower houses the "Bells of Congress" and offers panoramic views of the city and its surroundings on an observation level. At the time of its completion, the Post Office Building contained the largest uninterrupted enclosed space in the city. In 2013 the U.S. General Services Administration (GSA) leased the property for 60 years to a consortium headed by "DJT Holdings LLC" and they developed the property into a luxury hotel and the Trump International Hotel Washington, D.C., which opened in September 2016.

Notice the Statue in front of the Old Post Office and Clock Tower, of Ben Franklin, United States' first Post Master General.

Here is an excerpt of Ben Franklin's appeal for prayer at the Constitutional Convention.

"In this situation of this Assembly, groping as it were in the dark to find political truth, and scarce able to distinguish it when presented to us, how has it happened, Sir, that we have not hitherto once thought of humbly applying to the Father of lights to illuminate our understandings? In the beginning of the Contest with G. Britain, when we were sensible of danger we had daily prayer in this room for the divine protection. Our prayers, Sir, were heard, and they were graciously answered. All of us who were engaged in the struggle must have observed frequent instances of a Superintending Providence in our favor. To that kind Providence we owe this happy

opportunity of consulting in peace on the means of establishing our future national felicity.

And have we now forgotten that powerful Friend? I have lived, Sir, a long time, and the longer I live, the more convincing proofs I see of this truth- that God governs in the affairs of men. And if a sparrow cannot fall to the ground without his notice, is it probable that an empire can rise without his aid? We have been assured, Sir, in the sacred writings, that "except the Lord build the House they labour in vain that build it. I firmly believe this; and I also believe that without his concurring aid we shall succeed in this political building no better than the Builders of Babel:

We shall be divided by our little partial local interests; our projects will be confounded, and we ourselves shall become a reproach and bye word down to future ages. And what is worse, mankind may hereafter from this unfortunate instance, despair of establishing Governments by

Human Wisdom and leave it to chance, war and conquest."

Although noble in suggestion, the idea failed to pass as the delegates could not agree on how to pay the invited pastor to lead them in prayer.

Did you know?

You can take the elevator to the top of the Old Post Office Pavillion for a magnificent view of Washington, D.C. Enter from the ground floor next to the Starbucks, follow the hall past the gift store to the elevators that take you to the top.

Site: Temperance Fountain

Metro Stop: Navy Memorial Blue/ Orange/ Silver Lines Archives

The Temperance Fountain is a fountain and statue located in Washington, D.C., donated to the city in 1882 by Henry D. Cogswell, a dentist from San Francisco, California, who was

a crusader in the temperance movement. This fountain was one of a series of temperance fountains he designed and commissioned in a belief that easy access to cool drinking water would keep people from consuming alcoholic beverages. The fountain has four stone columns

supporting a canopy on whose sides the words "Temperance," "Faith," "Hope," "Charity," are chiseled. I Corinthians 13:13 "And now abideth faith, hope, charity, these three; but the greatest of these is charity."

Atop this canopy is a life-sized heron, and the centerpiece is a pair of entwined heraldic scaly dolphins. Originally, visitors were supposed to freely drink ice water flowing from the dolphins' snouts with a brass cup attached to the fountain and the overflow was collected by a trough for horses.

Site FDR's original memorial

Metro Stop: Archives Station Blue/ Orange Silver Lines

The plaque near this sign is pretty amusing to me, it reads "In September of 1941 Franklin Delano Roosevelt called his friend Supreme Court Justice Frankfurter to the White House and asked the Justice to remember the wish he then expressed: If any memorial is erected to me, I know exactly what I would like it to be. I should like it to consist of a block about the size of this (putting his hand on his desk) and placed in the center of that green plot in front of the Archives Building. I don't care what it is made of, limestone or granite or whatnot. But I want it plain without any ornamentation with the simple carving 'In memory of _____ .'" (That is funny.)

Site: World War II Memorial

Metro Stop: Smithsonian Blue/ Orange Silver Lines

World War II is often described as 'the last great war' and by that often they mean it was the last war that the sides were clearly defined between good and evil. The spirit of the age

captured this clearly in the military service recruiting posters.

The memorial's announcement stone reads, "Here in the presence of Washington and Lincoln, one the 18th century father and the other the 19th century preserver of our nation, we honor those 20th century Americans who took up the struggle during the Second World War and made the sacrifices to perpetuate the gift our forefathers entrusted to us: a nation conceived in liberty and justice."

The imposing memorial at the National Mall here honors not only the hundreds of thousands of Americans who lost their lives on the battlefields of Europe, the Pacific and East Asia, but also the millions who fought and returned home, and those who supported them. It also honors millions of women who performed "men's jobs" in factories and other places to free men for the battlefield and to keep America running.(7)

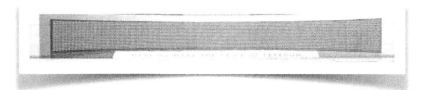

The "Freedom Wall Field of Gold Stars" is graced with gold stars commemorating more than 400,000 Americans who gave their lives in the war. The inscription sums up the memorial's meaning: "Here we mark the price of freedom."

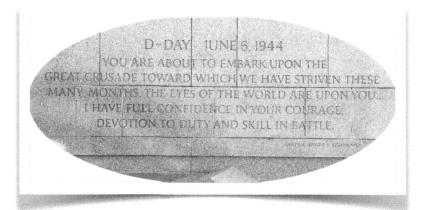

Only two defining forces have ever offered to die for you: Jesus Christ and the United States Soldier. One died for your soul; the other for your freedom. Truly in America we are blessed with freedom, the freedom that comes at the expense of others.

One item of note is on the North side of the memorial etched with words from Army Gen. George C. Marshall and Army Gen. Dwight D. Eisenhower. On D-Day, June 6, 1944, Eisenhower said, "You are about to embark upon the great crusade toward which we have striven these many months."

Look behind the memorial for Kilroy- the ubiquitous graffiti left everywhere by the WWII GI. The US History Channel broadcast *Fort Knox: Secrets Revealed* in 2007 included a shot of a chalked "KILROY WAS HERE" dated 1937-05-13. Fort Knox's vault was loaded in 1937 and inaccessible until the 1970s, when an audit was carried out and the footage was shot. According to one story, German intelligence found the phrase on captured American equipment. This led Adolf Hitler to believe that Kilroy could be the name or codename of a high-level Allied spy. At the time of the Potsdam Conference in 1945, it was rumored that Stalin found "Kilroy was here" written in the VIP bathroom, prompting him to ask his aides who Kilroy was.

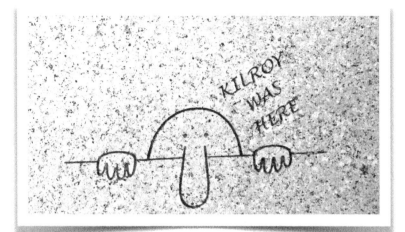

Did you know?

- On the floor of the Memorial Arches is the
  WWII victory medal surrounded by the years
  "1941-1945" and the words "Victory on Land,"
  "Victory at Sea," and "Victory in the Air."
- Circling the plaza are 56 granite pillars – one for
  each of the states, territories, and the District of
  Columbia – connected by a bronze sculpted
  rope celebrating the unity of the nation.

Text of Radio Address - Prayer on D-Day, June 6, 1944:

"My fellow Americans: Last night, when I spoke with you about the fall of Rome, I knew at that moment that troops of the United States and our allies were crossing the Channel in another and greater operation. It has come to pass with success thus far.

And so, in this poignant hour, I ask you to join with me in prayer:

Almighty God: Our sons, pride of our Nation, this day have set upon a mighty endeavor, a struggle to preserve our Republic, our religion, and our civilization, and to set free a suffering humanity.

Lead them straight and true; give strength to their arms, stoutness to their hearts, steadfastness in their faith.

They will need Thy blessings. Their road will be long and hard. For the enemy is strong. He may hurl back our forces. Success may not come with rushing speed, but we shall return again and again; and we know that by Thy grace, and by the righteousness of our cause, our sons will triumph.

They will be sore tried, by night and by day, without rest-until the victory is won. The darkness will be rent by noise and flame. Men's souls will be shaken with the violences of war.

For these men are lately drawn from the ways of peace. They fight not for the lust of conquest. They fight to end conquest. They fight to liberate. They fight to let justice arise, and tolerance and good will among all Thy people. They yearn but for the end of battle, for their return to the haven of home.

Some will never return. Embrace these, Father, and receive them, Thy heroic servants, into Thy kingdom.

And for us at home -- fathers, mothers, children, wives, sisters, and brothers of brave men overseas — whose thoughts and prayers are ever with them--help us, Almighty God, to rededicate ourselves in renewed faith in Thee in this hour of great sacrifice.

Many people have urged that I call the Nation into a single day of special prayer. But because the road is long and the desire is great, I ask that our people devote themselves in a continuance of prayer. As we rise to each new day, and again when each day is spent, let words of prayer be on our lips, invoking Thy help to our efforts.

Give us strength, too -- strength in our daily tasks, to redouble the contributions we make in the physical and the material support of our armed forces.

And let our hearts be stout, to wait out the long travail, to bear sorrows that may come, to impart our courage unto our sons wheresoever they may be.

And, O Lord, give us Faith. Give us Faith in Thee; Faith in our sons; Faith in each other; Faith in our united crusade. Let not the keenness of our spirit ever be dulled. Let not the impacts of temporary events, of temporal matters of but fleeting moment let not these deter us in our unconquerable purpose.

With Thy blessing, we shall prevail over the unholy forces of our enemy. Help us to conquer the apostles of greed and racial arrogancies. Lead us to the saving of our country, and with our sister Nations into a world unity that will spell a sure peace a peace invulnerable to the schemings of unworthy men. And a peace that will let all of men live in freedom, reaping the just rewards of their honest toil.

Thy will be done, Almighty God. Amen."

Did you know?

- President Roosevelt encouraged Bible reading among our armed forces and dedicated a New Testament for the men and women in uniform.

Site Korean War memorial.

Metro Stops Smithsonian, Foggy Bottom, Blue/ Orange/ SilverLines or Blue Line Arlington

Nineteen stainless steel statues were sculpted by Frank Gaylord are approximately seven feet tall and represent an ethnic cross section of America. The advance party has 14 Army, three Marine, one Navy and one Air Force members.

The statues stand in patches of Juniper bushes and are separated by polished granite strips, which give a semblance of order and symbolize the rice paddies of Korea. The troops wear ponchos covering their weapons and equipment. The ponchos seem to blow in the cold winds of Korea. Original design plans called for 38 soldiers representing the 38th parallel separating North and South Korea. With funding running tight they settled on 19 soldiers and a black granite mural, highly polished to reflect the 19 soldiers thereby giving the desired effect of 38. The memorial commemorates the sacrifices of the 5.8 million Americans who served in the U.S. armed services during the three-year period of the Korean War. The war was one of the most hard fought in our history. During its relatively short duration from June 25, 1950 to July 27, 1953, 36,574 Americans died in hostile actions in the Korean War theater. Of these, 8,200 are listed as missing in action or lost or buried at sea. In addition, 103,284 were wounded during the conflict.

Korean War Memorial Statue Key**

Position	Service	Duty	Weapon
1	Army	Lead Scout	M-1
2	Army	Scout	M-1
3	Army	Squad Leader	M-1
4	Army	BAR Man	BAR *
5	Army	BAR Assistant	Carbine
6	Army	Rifleman	M-1
7	Army	Group Leader	Carbine
8	Army	Radio Operator	Carbine
9	Army	Army Medic	None
10	Army	Forward Observer	Carbine
11	USAF	Air-Ground Controller	Carbine
12	USMC	Assistant Gunner	Tripod
13	USMC	Gunner	Machine Gun
14	Navy	Corpsman	None
15	USMC	Gunner	M-1
16	Army	Rifleman	M-1
17	Army	Rifleman	M-1
18	Army	Asst. Group leader	M-1
19	Army	Rifleman	M-1

*

* * Browning Automatic Rifle   **Chart: koreanwarvetsmemorial.org

OUR NATION HONORS
HER SONS AND DAUGHTERS
WHO ANSWERED THE CALL
TO DEFEND A COUNTRY
THEY NEVER KNEW
AND A PEOPLE
THEY NEVER MET

1950 ▾ KOREA ▾ 1953

Site: Vietnam War Memorial

Metro Stops: Smithsonian, Foggy Bottom, Blue/ Orange/ SilverLines or Arlington Blue Line

This Memorial was built without any government funds. When you look upon the wall, your reflection can be seen simultaneously with the 58,318 engraved names, which is meant to symbolically bring the past and present together. One wall points toward the Washington Monument, the other in the direction of the Lincoln Memorial. The names are listed in chronological order based on the date of casualty, and within each day, names are shown in alphabetical order.

The first names appear at the center of the wall at the top of panel 1E. The panels are filled like pages of a journal listing the men and women's names as they fell. Upon reaching the farthest east end of the memorial at panel 70E, the pattern continues from the far west end of the memorial at panel 70W, continuing back to the center at

Organization of Vietnam Veterans Memorial

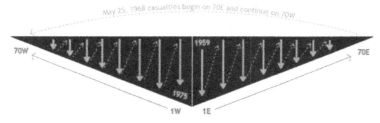

Names are listed chronologically by date of casualty in the pattern shown, beginning in 1959 on panel 1E.

May 25, 1968 casualties begin on 70E and continue on 70W

70W   70E

1959

1975

1W   1E

By referencing a printed or online registry, the panel numbers may be used to locate a name on the wall.

panel 1W. In this manner, the memorial evokes a theme of closure or completion; the first are with the last.(8)

Many visitors leave sentimental items, wedding announcements, rings, and military paraphernalia at the memorial, these items are gathered by park staff. Non-perishable items are archived in a storage facility.

One of the largest things left was a 1960's era Harley Davidson Chopper left by "the People of Wisconsin." Early one morning, Duery Felton, curator of the Vietnam Veterans Memorial Collection [the objects left at The Wall], got an urgent call from a Park Ranger. "Some fools have left a motorcycle at The Wall," the ranger said.

Over the years, the bike has also traveled to events across the country, most recently back to Wisconsin in May 2010 for a large veteran event.

While back in the neighborhood, the bike got new tires, some paint touch up and a detailed cleaning.(9)

Looking east you have a clear view of the Washington Monument. If you are looking for a

name on the wall, printed registries are available at the memorial. They are organized alphabetically by last name. Electronic registries available online or accessible by park staff in the information kiosk at the memorial allow users to search by several data including first name, last name, branch of service, rank, date of birth, date of casualty, state and/or city where they enlisted. Registry entries include a panel number and row number that correspond to its location in the memorial (see graphic p.138). Panel numbers are engraved in the memorial at the bottom of each panel. For row number, count down from the highest row on the panel. Each row contains five names (six where a name has been added since the wall was originally installed).

Some visitors take pictures. Some just want to touch and see the names. For others, they bring home what's commonly called a "rubbing." Rub a marker or crayon over a piece of paper atop the name and you have a lasting memory - a perfect image of the name as it appears. When Vietnam veterans visit the memorial, the rubbings are more than a name on paper, they are memories of the fallen. "He was from my hometown" is not an uncommon sentiment.

The Three Soldiers statue sits a few feet from the Vietnam Veterans Memorial Wall. This statue was added after the Wall opened to complement it and to offer an alternative memorial for critics who disliked the non-traditional design of the Wall. The sculpture's three soldiers represent the diversity of the US military by including a Caucasian, African American, and Latino American whose service branch is intentionally ambiguous. Together, they face the Wall as if they are looking for a fallen buddy.

With no fanfare or public notice – 265,000 women volunteered to go where they were needed, to do what was needed. During the Vietnam War, these young women, most in their 20s, risked their lives to care for our country's wounded and dying. Their humanity and compassion equalled their lifesaving and comforting skills. It is a sculpture in the round portraying three Vietnam-era women, one of whom is praying (not visible in the picture) one of whom is looking for a medivac helicopter and one of whom is caring for a wounded male. Some tour guides refer to these nurses as representing Faith, Hope, and Charity.

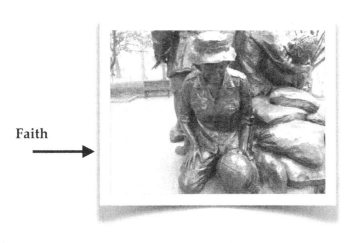

Faith

Hope

Charity

145

Site: **Ronald Reagan International Trade Center**

Metro Stop: Federal Triangle on the Blue, Silver and Orange Lines

What to look for: The Ronald Reagan Building and International Trade Center, named after former United States President Ronald Reagan, is located in downtown Washington, D.C., and was the first federal building in Washington designed for both governmental and private sector purposes. On the outside, it looks like one of Washington, D.C.'s grand federal buildings but on the inside, it couldn't be more... well, unfederal! Along the front of the building on 14th Street between Constitution Ave. and Pennsylvania Ave. you will see the Liberty of Worship Statue and she is holding two tablets representing the Ten Commandments.

Site: White House

Metro Stops: McPherson or Farragut Blue/ Orange, Silver lines

The White House is the official residence and workplace of the President of the United States. It is located at 1600 Pennsylvania Avenue NW in Washington, D.C. and has been the residence of every U.S. President since John Adams in 1800. The term "White House" is often used as a metonym for the president and his advisers.

John Adams' blessing was carved into the state dining room mantel in 1945. This 1968 photograph by White House Photographer Michael Geissinger is of John Adams' blessing, which is engraved in the mantel in the State Dining Room. The benediction reads, "I Pray Heaven To Bestow The Best Of Blessings On This House And All that shall hereafter Inhabit it. May none but Honest and Wise Men ever rule under This Roof." The words are taken from a letter written to Abigail Adams from the President's House by Adams in 1800.

Site: Willard Hotel 1401 Pennsylvania Avenue NW

Metro Stop: Federal Triangle on the Blue, Silver and Orange Lines

Upon hearing a Union regiment singing "John Brown's Body" as they marched beneath her window, Julia Ward Howe wrote the lyrics to "The Battle Hymn of the Republic" while staying at the hotel in November 1861. A plaque, located on the Pennsylvania Ave. side of the hotel, commemorates this effort.

Site: National Law Enforcement Officers Memorial

Metro Stop: Judiciary Square Red Line

The National Law Enforcement Officers Memorial in Washington, D.C., United States, at Judiciary Square, honors 21,100+ U.S. law enforcement officers who have died in the line of duty throughout American history. The memorial features four bronze lions--two male and two female—each watching over a pair of lion cubs.

(photo by Dan Yglesias)

"The wicked flee when no man pursueth, but the righteous are as bold as a lion." Proverbs 28:1

Site: Statue of John Witherspoon
Metro Stop: Dupont Circle Red Line

John Witherspoon, Signer of the Declaration of Independence, was a Presbyterian minister and during his lifetime considered a reformer, statesman, scholar, political activist, confidant of George Washington, seen holding his Bible.

Site: Martin Luther Monument
Metro Site: Dupont Circle Red Line
McPherson Square Blue/ Orange/ Silver Lines

The **Luther Monument** is a public artwork located at Luther Place Memorial Church in Washington, D.C., United States. The monument to Martin Luther, the theologian and Protestant Reformer, is a bronze full-length portrait. It is a

copy of the Luther Monument in Worms, Germany. Martin Luther stands dressed in long robes with his proper right leg moving slightly forward. The sculpture, which shows an excommunicated Luther defending himself during his trial before the Diet of Worms in 1521, features Luther resting his proper right hand on top of a large Bible that he holds in his proper left hand. "Here I stand" pose, his hair curls around his face and he looks outward, and slightly upward. Martin Luther, at his trial called the Diet of Worms said that if his writings were proven to be false by Scripture, then he himself would burn his own books. Johann von Eck asked him to give a straighter answer. Give us a direct answer, he demanded, "without horns."

Martin Luther answered in two languages:

"Unless I am refuted and convicted by testimonies of the Scriptures or by clear arguments (since I believe neither the Pope nor the Councils alone; it being evident that they have often erred and contradicted themselves), I am conquered by the Holy Scriptures quoted by me, and my conscience is bound in the word of God: I can not and will not recant any thing, since it is unsafe and dangerous to do any thing against the conscience. Here I stand! I cannot do otherwise. God help me! Amen."(10)

Martin Luther on Education:
"Every institution, where the Word of God is not taught regularly, must fail. That is why we observe the kind of people who are now and will continue to be in the universities . . . I greatly fear that the universities are but wide-open gates leading to hell, as they are not diligent in training and impressing the Holy Scripture on the young students."

Site: Jefferson Building Library of Congress
Metro Stop: Capitol South Blue, Orange & Silver Lines

The Library of Congress is the largest library in the world, with millions of books, recordings, photographs, newspapers, maps and manuscripts in its collections. The Library is the main research arm of the U.S. Congress and the home of the U.S. Copyright Office. The Library preserves and provides access to a rich, diverse and enduring source of knowledge to inform, inspire and engage everyone.(11) In addition to being a national treasure architecturally, it houses an impressive collection of spiritual heritage to celebrate on your tour.

The Apostle St. Paul, the Main Reading Room.

Moses overlooking the Main Reading Room.

The Statue *Religion* in the Main Reading Room.

Micah 6:8 over the Statue of Religion.

Shakespeare, *As You Like It*, Act ii, Scene 1
Sermons in Stones are like Stories in Stones.

Good Religion originating in Judea, the figure to the left is wearing the Urim and Thummim stones.

The West Corridor John 1:5

The North Corridor Proverbs 4:7

The Gutenberg Bible is the first great book printed in Western Europe from movable metal type. This Bible, with its noble Gothic type richly impressed on the page, is recognized as a masterpiece of fine printing and craftsmanship and is all the more remarkable because it was undoubtedly one of the very first books to emerge from the press.

Gutenberg's invention of the mechanical printing press made it possible for the accumulated knowledge of the human race to become the common property of every person who knew how to read—an immense forward step in the emancipation of the human mind.

Johann Gutenberg, (1400 - 1468) is credited for inventing the process of making uniform and interchangeable metal types and for solving the many problems of finding the right materials and methods for printing. The Library of Congress copy is printed entirely on vellum, a fine parchment made from animal skin, and is one of only three perfect vellum copies known to exist. It is valued at $25,000,000.(12)

Early Printers printing a Bible and inspecting their work.

Site: Union Station

Metro Site: Union Station Red Line

Washington Union Station is one of the country's first great union railroad terminals. Designed by renowned architect, Daniel Burnham, the station opened on October 27, 1907 and was completed in April 1908.

During its heyday in the early 1940's, Union Station was a thriving transportation hub serving up to 42,000 passengers daily. After 1945, conditions deteriorated quickly. The demand on transportation during World War II wore greatly on the station, and repairs were often done inexpensively, diminishing the station's elegance. Public trends shifted from rail to cars and planes for long-distance travel, which further diminished rail passenger revenues, station activity and the feeling of excitement that once percolated through the building.

In the late 1950s, the Station's owners began searching for an alternative use. In 1964, the District of Columbia designated the building as an historic landmark and in 1969 it was listed in the National Register of Historic Places; Columbus Plaza, located in the front of the station, was listed in 1980. During the mid-1960s, the federal government took over the building for use as a new National Visitor Center. However, a lack of funding for the conversion, poor design and changing tastes made it a failure soon after it opened in 1976. Union Station's low point came in 1981 when a driving rain sent pieces of the ceiling, already damaged by a leaky roof, crashing down into the main waiting room.(13) As you walk out the front of Union Station you will see a

reproduction of the Liberty Bell. Notice the Bible verse ringing the top of the Liberty Bell.

Proclaim Liberty throughout the land unto all the inhabitants thereof. Leviticus 25:10

The Pennsylvania Assembly ordered the Bell in 1751 to commemorate the 50-year anniversary of William Penn's 1701 Charter of Privileges, Pennsylvania's original Constitution. It speaks of the rights and freedoms valued by people the world over. Particularly forward thinking were Penn's ideas on religious freedom, his liberal stance on Native American rights, and his inclusion of citizens in enacting laws. The

Liberty Bell gained iconic importance when abolitionists in their efforts to put an end to slavery throughout America adopted it as a symbol. As the Bell was created to commemorate the golden anniversary of Penn's Charter, the quotation "Proclaim Liberty throughout all the land unto all the inhabitants thereof," from Leviticus 25:10, was particularly apt. For the line in the Bible immediately preceding "proclaim liberty" is, "And ye shall hallow the fiftieth year." What better way to pay homage to Penn and hallow the 50th year than with a bell proclaiming liberty?(14)

Abolitionists rallied around "Proclaim Liberty throughout all the land unto all the inhabitants thereof," in their fight against slavery. The Liberty Bell's inscription conveys a message of liberty, which goes beyond the words themselves.

Amusingly in 1976, the Procrastinators Club petitioned Whitechapel Foundry in England with their notice of a crack in the Liberty Bell saying "We got a lemon, what about the warranty?" Whitechapel Foundry stood by their work and replied they would "be happy to replace the cracked bell as long as they returned it in the original packaging."

165

As you are standing in front of the reproduction of the Liberty Bell, turn around and look at the front of Union Station. You will notice the last line of each inscription is a Bible verse.

Thou hast put all things under his feet. Psalm 8:6

The desert shall rejoice and blossom as a rose.
Isaiah 35:1

The Truth shall make you free. John 8:32

Site: Museum of the Bible

Metro Stop: Federal Center SW Blue /Orange or Silver Lines

The Museum of the Bible documents the narrative, history and impact of the Bible. The museum opened on November 17, 2017. With 1,150 items from the museum's permanent collection and 2,000 items on loan from other institutions and collections, the museum claims to have amassed one of the largest assemblies of biblical artifacts and texts in the world through collaborations with private donors, institutions, and other museums. Each of the floors in the museum contains a different exhibit which emphasizes different aspects of the Bible's history or impact. This includes three permanent exhibit floors, each measuring 55,000 square feet.

The first floor combines ancient artifacts with modern technology meant to immerse the

participant in the Bible. The front entrance on 4th Street SW features 40-foot tall, 2.5 tons bronze front doors with stained glass art containing a relief depicting the creation account in Genesis. There is also a grand lobby with a 200-foot LED ceiling allowing for changing visual effects and messages.

The second floor focuses on the Bible's impact on world culture, in areas like science, justice, and freedom. Another section is dedicated to the Bible's impact in American history.

The third floor presents the general narrative of the Bible from Abraham through the creation of Israel to the ministry of Jesus and the early church. This floor also contains a large Jewish Bible section.

The fourth floor presents biblical history and archaeology. The museum "will not whitewash conflicts in Christian history but will explain the arguments that were made at the time."

The fifth level contains a performing arts theater with a 500-person amphitheater. The museum plans to sponsor scholarly lectures as well as multimedia performances relating to the

Bible. The fifth floor also contains separate exhibit space for displays presented by the Israel Antiquities Authority. (15)

I think the greatest blessing of having the Museum of the Bible in Washington, D.C. is that you have a six story building dedicated to the Bible's influence on culture. Not long ago, you would be hard pressed to find an open English Bible in any government building. There was the Gutenburg Bible, and the Mainz Bible in the Library of Congress Jefferson Building, but no open English Bible. That was ironic because the Library of Congress houses one of the largest collection of rare books and rare copies of the Bible.

Did you know?

- Newsweek magazine, December 27, 1982, "How the Bible Made America," made this revealing statement, "historians are discovering that the Bible, perhaps even more than the Constitution, is our Founding document.

Site: Rosslyn Metro stop

Orange & Blue Lines

Most stops in Washington, D.C are for a spiritual heritage site or an American History site. This one is just fun. The average mall escalator is 15 feet long. This escalator is 194 feet long. The longest in the world is the Moscow Metro station at Park Pobedy, 413 feet long. This stop is typically on our normal tour so it is one more thing to experience that we don't normally see back home.

Site: Mount Vernon

Eleven miles south of Washington, D.C. on the George Washington Parkway

George Washington – first American president, commander of the Continental Army, president of the Constitutional Convention, and gentleman planter. Mount Vernon is the place to learn more about the many varied roles that George Washington excelled in and tremendous

legacy that he left for America and the World.(16) The estate is situated on the banks of the Potomac River in Fairfax County, Virginia, near Alexandria, across from Prince George's County, Maryland.

George Washington's Bible

The Washington family had owned land in the area since the time of Washington's great-grandfather in 1674. Around 1734 they embarked on an expansion of the estate that continued under George Washington, who began leasing the estate in 1754, but did not become its sole owner until 1761. In 1858, Washington sold the mansion and a portion of the estate's land to the Mount Vernon Ladies' Association. The Association paid the final installment of the purchase price of $200,000 ($5,714,300.+ in today's dollars) on 9 December 1859, taking possession on 22 February 1860. The estate served as a neutral ground for both sides during the American Civil War, although fighting raged across the nearby countryside. Troops from both the Union and the Confederacy toured the building. The two women caretakers asked that the soldiers leave their arms behind and either change to civilian clothes or at least cover their uniforms. They usually did as asked.(16)

The mansion has been fully restored by the Mount Vernon Ladies' Association, independent of the US government, with no tax dollars expended to support the 500-acre estate, its educational programs or activities. Because of this fact, Mount Vernon is not hostage to political correctness and can tell the truth about George Washington. As you tour the estate and watch the programs, note how many times Divine Providence is mentioned by General Washington. While living at Mount Vernon, the Washingtons had a pew and attended services at nearby Pohick

Church in Truro Parish in Fairfax County. While in the educational section you can see a reproduction of the Washington Pew at Pohick Church.

George Washington died at Mount Vernon on December 14, 1799. His last will outlined his desire to be buried at home at Mount Vernon. Washington additionally made provisions for a new brick tomb to be constructed after his death, which would replace the original yet quickly deteriorating family burial vault. In 1831, Washington's body was transferred to the new tomb, along with the remains of Martha

Washington and other family members. Today, the gently wooded enclosure that surrounds the Washingtons' final resting place is a lovely, fitting space to pay homage to the Father of Our Country and the first First Lady.(17)

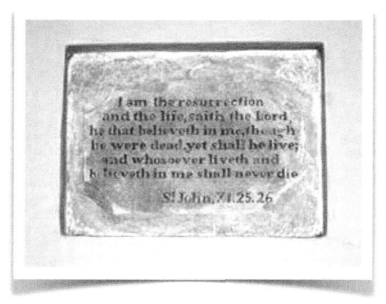

The Bible Verse in the back of Washington's Tomb.

Site: John Wesley Statue American University
Metro Stop: Tenleytown / AU Red Line

John Wesley arrived in the colony of Georgia in February 1736. On Thursday July 1, 1736 Wesley records in his diary, "The Indians had audience: Chicali, their head man dined with Mr. Oglethorpe. After dinner, I asked the grey-headed old man what he thought he was made for. He said 'He that is above knows what He made us for. We know nothing. We are in the dark. But White man know much. And yet white man build great houses, as if they were to live forever. But

179

white man cannot live forever. In a little time, white men will be dust as well as I.' I told him, 'If

red men will learn the Good Book, they may know as much as white men. But neither we nor you can understand that Book unless we are taught by Him that is above: and He will not teach you unless you avoid what you already know is not good.' He answered, 'I believe that. He will not teach us while our hearts are not white. And our men do what they know is not good: they kill their own children. And our women do what they know is not good: they kill the child before it is born. Therefore He that is above does not send us the good book.'" This is the first reference to abortion in American Literature.

Wesley was a keen abolitionist, speaking out and writing against the slave trade. He published a pamphlet on slavery, titled *Thoughts Upon Slavery*, in 1774. He wrote, "Liberty is the right of every human creature, as soon as he breathes the vital air; and no human law can deprive him of that right which he derives from the law of nature." Wesley influenced George Whitefield, John Newton and William Wilberforce, who were also influential in the abolition of slavery in Britain.

Site: Statue of the Prophet Daniel at the Organization of American States
Metro Stops: Federal Triangle, McPherson Square
Orange / Blue / Silver Lines

The eight-foot statue depicts the Prophet Daniel. Nearly all that is known about him is derived from the book of Daniel making that book more than a treasure of prophetic literature but painting a picture of Daniel as a man of God. The Scrolling in his right hand says this is Daniel.

Site: Rabonni Statue Rock Creek Cemetery

John 20:16 *Jesus saith unto her, Mary. She turned herself, and saith unto him, Rabboni; which is to say, Master.* (KJV)

Rabboni is a public artwork by American artist Gutzon Borglum, located in Rock Creek Cemetery in Washington, D.C., United States. *Rabboni* was surveyed as part of the Smithsonian *Save Outdoor Sculpture!* survey in 1993. This

Realist sculpture depicts Mary Magdalene emerging from an alcove consisting of three granite blocks that surround her. Dressed in long robes and a cape which covers her head, her right hand is raised to lift the cape from her head. Her left arm is extended outward in front of her. Her

right leg is stepping forward, to recognize Jesus Christ has risen from his tomb on Easter. The front of the sculptures base is inscribed: RABBONI

On the back of the center granite piece is an upper bronze plaque which is inscribed:

THE END OF BIRTH IS DEATH
THE END OF DEATH IS LIFE AND
WHERFOR MOURNEST THOU (19)

Site: Meditation Rock Fredricksburg, VA

Here Mary Ball Washington prayed for the safety of her son and country during the dark days of the revolution. In 1772 Mary Washington

moved from "Ferry Farm" to a house in Fredericksburg bought by her son, George Washington. She often came to this spot to meditate and to pray and requested that she be buried here. Mary Washington died in 1789 and her grave went unmarked for many years. In 1833, Silas Burrows, a wealthy New York merchant, agreed to pay for a monument for

Mary Washington's grave and President Jackson laid the cornerstone. In 1889, the centennial year of Mary Washington's death, The National Mary Washington Memorial Association erected the present monument and on May 10, 1894, it was dedicated. President Grover Cleveland was the honored guest and main speaker. Vice President Adlai E. Stevenson, the Governor of Virginia and other dignitaries were present.(20)

Site: George H.W.Bush Center for Intelligence

Headquarters of the Central Intelligence Agency, located in the unincorporated community of Langley in Fairfax County, Virginia, United States; near to Washington, D.C.

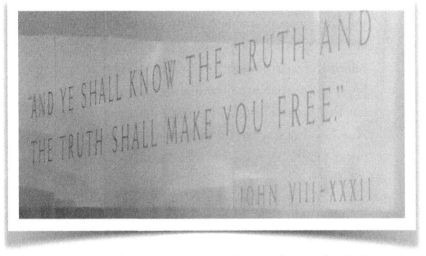

"And Ye Shall Know the Truth and the Truth Shall Make You Free"   John 8:32

Epilogue:

Often after a presentation on Stories in Stones, I will hear someone say something to the effect that "I went to Washington, D.C. and took a tour and our tour guide didn't mention one thing that you spoke of this evening. Why do you think that is?" My thought to myself is, the reason the secularists can't find the Bible verses on the monuments is the same reason that a crook can't find a cop, they are not looking too hard." But then I have to remind myself that part of the reason is that they have a big story to tell and a short time to tell it, so they can't possibly include everything. Another thought would be that maybe they were never taught or trained to look for these things.

Until recently, the Capitol tours given by some of the congressional office staff that I have overheard were not really up to speed. Sterile, godless and majoring on the minor, thick with thin things. Rarely was so little true history compressed into so many words and so many steps around the Capitol Building. Truly , to quote Gertrude Stein, "there was no there there."

Whoever assembled their script imagined the history and architectural beauty of our nation's Capitol to be full of fluid possibilities. Plenty of innuendo, paltry on insight, and abundant in public mediocrity. I've often felt sorry for the poor souls on one of their "tours."

Will there ever be another monument with a Bible verse on it or a monument to a man or woman with a clear Christian testimony? I don't know. It all depends on who controls the narrative and what kind of nation we wish to project ourselves to be.

"Time has forever barred the way.

We can't return to yesterday.

Out of reach, beyond the blue.

Tomorrow waits in vain for you.

So take today, enjoy its measure.

Soon it will be yesterday's treasure."

Bonus Section

Over the next few pages are the rough text and amplification of the thoughts that I share with groups when we tour the Lincoln Memorial. Many of the insights you will find in the Lincoln Memorial section of this book.

Site: The Lincoln Memorial

Metro Stops: Foggy Bottom Georgetown on the Orange line or Arlington on the Blue line, either way, you have a walk to get there.

July 10, 1858 during the Lincoln Douglas debates:

"We are now a mighty nation; we are thirty, or about thirty, millions of people, and we own and inhabit about one-fifteenth part of the dry land of the whole earth. We run our memory back over the pages of history for about eighty-two years, and we discover that we were then a very small people in point of numbers, vastly inferior to what we are now, with a vastly less extent of country, with vastly less of everything we deem desirable among men; we look upon the change as exceedingly advantageous to us and to our posterity, and we fix upon something that happened away back, as in some way or other being connected with this rise of prosperity. We find a race of men living in that day whom we claim as our fathers and grandfathers; they were iron men; they fought for the principle that they were contending for; and we understood that by what they then did it has followed that the degree of prosperity which we now enjoy has come to us. We hold this annual celebration to remind ourselves of all the good done in this process of time, of how it was done and who did it, and how we are historically connected with it; and we go from these meetings in better humor with ourselves, we feel more attached the one to the other, and more firmly bound to the country we inhabit. In every way we are better men in the age, and race, and country in which we live, for these celebrations. But after we have done all this we have not yet reached the whole. There is something else connected with it. We have besides these, men descended by blood from our ancestors —among us, perhaps half our people, who are not descendants at all of these men; they are men who have come from Europe— German, Irish, French and Scandinavian— men that have come from Europe themselves, or whose ancestors have come hither and settled here, finding themselves our equals in all things. If they look back through this history to trace their connection with those days by blood, they find they have none, they cannot carry themselves back into that glorious epoch and make themselves feel that they are part of us, but when they look through that old Declaration of Independence, they find that those old men say that "We hold these truths to be self-evident, that all men are created equal;" and then they feel that that moral sentiment taught in that day evidences their relation to those men, that it is the father of all moral principle in them, and that they have a right to claim it as though they were blood of the blood, and flesh of the flesh, of the men who wrote that Declaration; and so they are. That is the electric cord in that Declaration that links the hearts of patriotic and liberty-loving men together, that will link those patriotic hearts as long as the love of freedom exists in the minds of men throughout the world."

This next fragment, referred to as *Meditation on the Divine Will,* was found and preserved by John Hay, one of President Lincoln's White House secretaries, who said it was not written to be seen of men. "The will of God prevails. In great contests each party claims to act in accordance with the will of God. Both may be, and one must be, wrong. God cannot be for and against the same thing at the same time. In the present civil war it is quite possible that God's purpose is something different from the purpose of either party -- and yet the human instrumentalities, working just as they do, are of the best adaptation to effect His purpose. I am almost ready to say that this is probably true -- that God wills this contest, and wills that it shall not end yet. By his mere great power, on the minds of the now contestants, He could have either saved or destroyed the Union without a human contest. Yet the contest began. And, having begun He could give the final victory to either side any day. Yet the contest proceeds."

Some of the thoughts expressed here, written after discouraging days of personal sorrow and military defeats, also appear in Lincoln's Second Inaugural Address of 1865.

Hay said that in this writing "Mr. Lincoln admits us into the most secret recesses of his soul .... Perplexed and afflicted beyond the power of human help, by the disasters of war, the wrangling of parties, and the inexorable and constraining logic of his own mind, he shut out the world one day, and tried to put into form his double sense of responsibility to human duty and Divine Power; and this was the result. It shows -- as has been said in another place -- the awful sincerity of a perfectly honest soul, trying to bring itself into closer communion with its Maker."

There are more books written about Lincoln than any other president. Some of the more notable ones are listed here.

Team of Rivals
Gospel at Gettysburg
Lincoln on Leadership
Lincoln in America
Killing Lincoln

After his death, like Washington, a cottage industry sprang up to cash in on his life. Traveling salesmen sold Lincoln Bibles. All they had was a lithograph of Lincoln on a front page.

Abraham Lincoln is born at the crossroads of America moving from an agrarian society to an industrial one.

Lincoln remains the only U.S. President to ever apply for a patent. He watched a produce barge get stranded on the Detroit River and suggested inflatable air chambers to free a grounded boat. Inflating the chambers lifted the boat.

When he was born we were still using the transportation of the Greeks and Romans, horse and buggy.

He rode to his inauguration in a steam powered train making him the first President to do so.

Four years after his death you could ride a train from St. Louis to California. When he was born, sea transportation was dependent on wind and sails. When he was President you could travel the Atlantic in ten days on a steam ship.

During Lincoln's lifetime merchants figured out to give a bag made of brown paper before they started shopping, for customer's convenience, allowing customers to carry more around the store before they purchased the products.

Some Notable inventions during Lincoln's lifetime:

- Cotton Gin
- Steel-tipped plow
- Elevator
- Ice box, to keep food cool with ice. (Prior to that, people used a root cellar with ice blocks.)
- Canning Jars
- Matches to keep the fire burning.
- Shoes were made to fit each foot.
- Pants were made with zippers, not just buttons.
- Levi Strauss made jeans from the fabric he was going to use to build ship sails and conestoga wagon covers.

Lincoln is attributed with the first known use of "Michigander." In 1848, he used it derisively to describe former Michigan Territorial Governor Lewis Cass. *Michiganian* is the preferred term for those who know.

During his lifetime the art of warfare advanced to the point of causing death and destruction in numbers unknown before. Rifling in barrels made rifles deadly accurate more so, than smooth bore muskets and round balls. Medical technology will not keep up. In Mount Morris, MI at Huckelberry Railroad the dentist's office has a field surgeon's kit for a doctor to serve in the Union Army. This kit consists of various meat saws for amputation, small flasks for whiskey for anesthesia, and lead balls, all with molar marks in them from the soldiers biting down on them as the surgeon operated.

During their lives, most men had three wives, two of whom, died in childbirth. People were fortunate if they had   two baths during summer, one during the winter. The doctors at Fort Mackinac learned that hot baths help to prevent disease. This is the world Lincoln is elected president to.

On February 11, 1861, newly elected President Abraham Lincoln delivered a Farewell Speech to his home state in Springfield, Illinois, as he left for Washington, D.C.: "I now leave, not knowing when or whether ever I may return, with a task before me greater than that which rested upon Washington. Without the assistance of that Divine Being who ever attended him, I cannot succeed. With that assistance I cannot fail. Trusting in Him who can go with me, and remain with you, and be everywhere for good, let us confidently hope that all will yet be well.... unless the great God who assisted him shall be with me and aid me, I must fail: but if the same omniscient mind and mighty arm that directed and protected him shall guide and support me, I shall not fail – I shall succeed. Let us all pray that the God of our fathers may not forsake us now. To him I commend you all. Permit me to ask that with equal sincerity and faith you will invoke his wisdom and guidance for me."

MARCH 4, 1861, 16th President Abraham Lincoln stated in his First Inaugural: "Intelligence, patriotism, Christianity, and a firm reliance on Him who has never yet forsaken this favored land, are still competent to adjust in the best way all our present difficulty."
The Civil War would kill 529,332 out of a population of 32 million, the modern day equivalent would be a war that kills 5,293,332.

On MARCH 30, 1863, President Abraham Lincoln proclaimed: "Whereas, it is the duty of nations as well as of men to own their dependence upon the overruling power of God, to confess their sins and transgressions in humble sorrow yet with assured hope that genuine repentance will lead to mercy and pardon, and to recognize the sublime truth, announced in the Holy Scriptures and proven by all history: that those nations only are blessed whose God is the Lord; And, insomuch as we know that, by His divine law, nations like individuals are subjected to punishments and chastisement in this world, may we not justly fear that the awful calamity of civil war, which now desolates the land may be but a punishment inflicted upon us for our presumptuous sins to the needful end of our national reformation as a whole people?

We have been the recipients of the choicest bounties of Heaven. We have been preserved these many years in peace and prosperity. We have grown in numbers, wealth and power as no other nation has ever grown. But we have forgotten God. We have forgotten the gracious Hand which preserved us in peace, and multiplied and enriched and strengthened us; and we have vainly imagined, in the deceitfulness of our hearts, that all these blessings were produced by some superior wisdom and virtue of our own. Intoxicated with unbroken success, we have become too self-sufficient to feel the necessity of redeeming and preserving grace, too proud to pray to the God that made us! It behooves us then to humble ourselves before the offended Power, to confess our national sins [the last President to say that we have committed national sins was Dwight D. Eisenhower. Ike 1953 mentioned our national sins, but he was quoting Lincoln] and to pray for clemency and forgiveness.

Now, therefore, in compliance with the request and fully concurring in the view of the Senate, I do, by this my proclamation, designate and set apart Thursday, the 30th day of April, 1863, as a day of national humiliation, fasting and prayer..."

October 1863 "I have wished that I was more devout than I am."

On Good Friday, April 14, 1865, President Abraham Lincoln agreed to go with his wife Mary Todd to Ford's Theatre as a way to escape the crowds of well-wishers coming to the White House. Ford's Theater on Tenth Street is a converted Baptist Church. After it burned to the ground in 1863, owner John Ford rebuilt it as a "magnificent thespian temple," replacing the pews with seats and transforming the deacons' stalls into private boxes. Upon completion, Ford's theater became the most state-of-the art theater in D.C. It is said that some good Baptists wagged their heads upon hearing of the former church burning to the ground - that's what you get for turning a church into a playhouse.

Rev. N.W. Miner, pastor of the First Baptist Church in Springfield Illinois, who was close to the Lincolns, recalled his conversation with Mrs. Lincoln about that fateful night of the assassination: "Mrs. Lincoln informed me that he seemed to take no notice of what was going on in the theater from the time he entered it till the discharge of the fatal pistol. She said that the last day he lived was the happiest of his life. The very last moments of his conscious life were spent in conversation with her about his future plans and what he wanted to do when his term of office expired. He said he wanted to visit the Holy Land and see those places hallowed by the footprints of the Saviour. He was saying there was no city he so much desired to see as Jerusalem. And with the words half spoken on his tongue, the bullet of the assassin entered the brain, and the soul of the great and good President was carried by the angels to the New Jerusalem above." We all know how President Abraham Lincoln was killed by John Wilkes Booth, but very few know of Lincoln's last wish to visit the Holy Land after his second term.

Atop the steps of this memorial will offer you a great view of the Reflecting Pool and the

Washington Monument. Inside this great memorial, note that over Abraham Lincoln's head they refer to this site as a Temple.

One notices that the statue of Lincoln can almost define his presidency in the manner of his body language. The left hand tight and the leg close to his body, the right hand open and the leg relaxed. As if the left side reflects the tension of the Civil War years and the right side, that brief moment of relief when the war ended.

On MAY 30, 1922, dedicating the Lincoln Memorial, Washington, D.C., President Warren G. Harding stated:

"In every moment of peril...there is the image of Lincoln to rivet our hopes and to renew our faith....He treasured the inheritance handed down by the founding fathers, the Ark of the Covenant wrought through their heroic sacrifices....Lincoln came almost as humbly as The Child of Bethlehem. His parents were unlettered, his home was devoid of every element of culture and refinement. He was no infant prodigy, no luxury facilitated or privilege hastened his development, but he had a God-given intellect, a love for work, a willingness to labor and a purpose to succeed."

Off to the side that is on Abraham Lincoln's right hand side you will see his Gettysburg Address. This short memorable speech mirrors the cadence of the King James Bible. Four score and seven years ago resonates like "Our Father which art in Heaven."

The brevity and poignancy makes this speech a classic for the ages. One writer wrote a book entitled the *Gospel at Gettysburg.* Lincoln says, 'the world will little note nor long remember what we say here.' There is historic irony right there, Famed orator of his day Edward Everett spoke for two hours before Lincoln and next to nobody knows it or remembers one word he said. Almost every school child can recite the parts of Lincoln's Gettysburg Address.

Note that he says, 'This Nation Under God.' There is a concerted effort in some quarters of our land to have any such reference removed from the public square.

The Phrase 'Government of the people, by the people, for the people' could be a paraphrase of Wycliffe's preface to his Bible.

Lincoln's attitude toward the Scriptures can be summed up in this quote, "In regard for this great book I have this to say, it is the best gift God has given to man. All the good Saviour gave to the world was communicated through this book."

On Abraham Lincoln's left hand side you will see his Second Inaugural Address.

On March 4, 1865, his Second Inaugural is the most theological statement in American History. One writer said these are the words of "America's Theologian of Anguish." This masterpiece of speech is replete with scriptural reference allusions containing numerous acknowledgments of God and citations of Bible verses, including the declarations that "we here highly resolve that . . . this nation under God . . . shall not perish from the earth"; "The Almighty has His own purposes. 'Woe unto the world because of offenses; for it must needs be that offenses come, but woe to that man by whom the offense cometh' (Matthew 18:7);" "as was said three thousand years ago, so still it must be said 'the judgments of the Lord are true and righteous altogether' (Psalms 19:9);" "one day every valley shall be exalted and every hill and mountain shall be made low, the rough places will be made plain, and the crooked places will be made straight and the glory of the Lord shall be revealed and all flesh see it together."

This address, given just 45 days before his assassination, President Abraham Lincoln states: "Neither party expected for the war the magnitude or the duration which it has already attained.... Both read the same Bible and pray to the same God, and each invokes His aid against the other. It may seem strange that any men should dare ask a just God's assistance in wringing their bread from the sweat of other men's faces, but let us judge not, that we be not judged. The prayers of both could not be answered. That of neither has been answered fully. The Almighty has His own purposes... If we shall suppose that American slavery is one of those offenses which, in the providence of God...He now wills to remove, and that He gives to both North and South this terrible war as the woe due to those by whom the offense came...so still it must be said 'the judgments of the Lord are true and righteous altogether.'" Lincoln expressed that he believed the Civil War was part of God's wrath on the sin of slavery.

In panel one of Lincoln's Second Inaugural Address, the mason was supposed to carve an "F" for the word Future and accidentally carved an

"E." Even though they tried to cover the mistake, it is still visible.

Aren't you thankful that when we make a mistake it isn't carved in stone?

President Calvin Coolidge, on May 25, 1924, at the Confederate Memorial in Arlington National Cemetery, Virginia, stated:

"It was Lincoln who pointed out that both sides prayed to the same God. When that is the case, it is only a matter of time when each will seek a common end. We can now see clearly what that end is. It is the maintenance of our American ideals, beneath a common flag, under the blessings of Almighty God."

During the early days of the Civil War, President Lincoln asked Michigan's wartime Governor Austin Blair for "not more than three regiments of troops." Michigan sent seven regiments. Three regiments went to the army on the Potomac and four guarded the Executive mansion. Looking out over the troops billeted in neat rows with evening campfires crackling on the South Lawn of the White House, a grateful Abraham Lincoln commented, "Thank God for Michigan."[20]

Tim Schmig lives with the love of his life, Sue, in the Historic
Mason District of Owosso, Michigan. They are occasionally
visited in their 1893 Victorian home by their four grandchildren
who are as much verbs as nouns.

Did I miss something? If you know of a site that needs to be included in future editions, feel free to contact me at timschmig@gmail.com

Like us on Facebook *Stories in Stones*

Please remember to phrase all questions in the form of a compliment.

"No people can be bound to acknowledge and adore the invisible hand which conducts the affairs of men more than the people of the United States." George Washington

"When the solution is simple, God is answering."

You can order Every Day is A Gift

Name_____

Address_____

City _____

State _____ Zip _____

$12.00 per copy. Please include $2 shipping/handling per book

and mail to   Sue Schmig

                 523 E. Mason St.

                 Owosso, MI 48867

Index of Contents

References

1 Ronald Reagan First Inaugural Address January 20, 1980

2 www.wbir.com

3 James BradleyÂ nativevillage.org

4 *Fundamentals of Prosperity*Â by Robert Babson, 1921

5 The Founders Bible.

6 Killing Lincoln, Bill O'Reilly p.104

7 Rudi Williams Armed Forces Press

8 Graphic fromÂ nps.gov

9 text and photo fromÂ history.net

10 (*History of the Christian Church*, vol. VII, ch. 3, sec. 55)

11 Carla Hayden Library of Congress

12 excerpted fromÂ loc.govÂ website

13 unionstationdc.com

14 history.org

15 excerpted from wikipedia

16 mountvernon.orgÂ

17 wikipedia

18 mountvernon.org

19 wikipedia

20 patch.com

Made in the USA
Columbia, SC
30 October 2020